THE 8 GREATEST MISTAKES

NEW MANAGERS MAKE

TOM DAVIDSON

Surviving Your Transition to a Leadership Position

RUMFORD
ACADEMY
PUBLISHING

RUMFORD
ACADEMY
PUBLISHING

Contact Rumford Academy Publishing
for individual or bulk orders at
info@davidsonleadership.com.

Graphic Design by Casler Design

The 8 greatest mistakes new managers make:
surviving your transition to a leadership position.

Printed in the United States of America
by Bang Printing
First Edition, Third Printing

ISBN 978-0-9844454-0-0

A FREE RIDE

Make your work your hobby –
   And ride, cowboy, ride!
Stick right in the saddle
   From dawn till eventide.
Make your work-time play-time –
   And join in with a zest!
Thus you'll learn work's meaning
   And what it means to rest.
Form the working habit –
   Then practice it with pride.
Make your work your hobby
   And ride it, cowboy, ride!

- Robert Harsha Davidson
  (1890-1983)

Rick,
Keep that disarming style
and I hope your
work is always your
hobby, too.

*"Those who cannot remember the past
are condemned to repeat it."*

– George Santayana (1863-1952)

Contents

Foreword

New managers constantly ask themselves, "How in the world should I handle this situation?" The answers are not always clear, so new managers try what feels "right" to them at the moment. Through trial and error, they eventually figure out what works and what doesn't. If only new managers could profit from others' past mistakes, the learning process would be so much faster.

The 8 Greatest Mistakes New Managers Make focuses on practical ways to avoid these mistakes. The author, Tom Davidson, combines 20 years of business background, 10 years of executive coaching, and his own personal experience transitioning from technical roles to leadership positions. He adds further depth to this project by including the insights of dozens of other successful leaders and coaches who have also learned the lessons of leadership the hard way. This is a raw look at the "been there, done that" experience of managers who have learned their lessons through years of experience, across many industries.

Tom Davidson has been part of the staff at Psychological Consultants, Inc. (PCI) for more than six years and has brought his experience, coaching, and training skills to our clients in a unique way. Since 1953, PCI has worked with

over 80,000 individuals, assessing their strengths and developmental needs, and providing feedback to help them become more effective in leadership roles. This book takes it one step further, and provides a useful "how-to" for individuals in that role. Tom identifies potential land mines, and artfully tells the reader how to bypass them, emerging more confident and authoritative in the managerial role.

Just as PCI has adapted its tools and technologies to accelerate the development of leaders, managers need to keep informed and remain agile in a changing workplace. This book will help them stay sharp as they do their part to mentor new talent and keep their organization's pipeline full of ready and willing leaders. Contemporary leaders must know what causes new managers to stumble so they can mitigate the fallout and accelerate the learning process.

This book is what you don't learn about managing in business school, *but desperately need to know*. The text goes beyond theory and tells you what works, what doesn't, and why. Tom's book should be required reading. Every new manager should read it; every leader seeking improvement should review it; and every manager of managers should embrace it as a reference tool. As a new or emerging manager, you will learn from the mistakes of others, so you can start with a "leg up" in your new role. As a current manager, you will gain fresh ideas to invigorate your approach to leadership.

You may be very successful in your current role. Others may have deemed you "a mover and a shaker" in the business. You may be ready to move up. You may even think you know it all. This book addresses those real-life leadership challenges that you don't yet know exist!

David C. Purdy, President
Psychological Consultants, Inc.
Richmond, Virginia

Acknowledgements

This is to thank the people who gave me life and inspired me to write this book. My parents provided me with the happiest childhood a kid could hope to have, including unconditional love, freedom to explore my interests, and three great brothers. For this, I am so very grateful to my parents, and this book is dedicated to the loving memory of Bob and Betty Davidson of Bethesda, Maryland.

Being the fourth of four boys had its distinct advantages, chief among them was learning from good role models – Bob, John and Bill – whom I love and admire deeply, each for their life's passions, services to humanity, choices of spouses, and amazing children and grandchildren.

I would like to thank all my managers, peers, and subordinates who have given my career context and meaning. Most recently, thanks to David Purdy and all my associates at Psychological Consultants, Inc. who have seen fit to include me in their important work.

About this book, I specifically want to thank the interviewees, some who are featured herein. It was their willingness to share their work experiences that gave this book its real-world perspective. I would also like to thank the following individuals for their varied contributions and

guidance, including: Debbie Barnett, Katie Casler, Ron Chapman, Bill Davidson, Bob Davidson, Dorothy Erlanger, Charlie Finley, Betsy Hill, Robert Holland, Cathy Lewis, Coleen Kenny, Conni Morse, Maggie Ruch, and Dave Winter. Without their help, this book would still be a dream and an unfulfilled promise.

The biggest thanks I reserve for my life partner, my one true love, my best friend, and my wife, Ellen, who inspires and nourishes me daily as we continue to navigate our lives together. I love you. Thank you for being you, for loving me, and for taking care of all the critters that always have and always will bring us so much joy.

- Tom Davidson

"If leaders don't learn to fail,
then they will fail to succeed."

–Tom Davidson

You Have to Fall to Climb

Learn to fail or fail to succeed

I learned to fall early. Growing up outdoors, I got to do everything from backpacking, canoeing, caving, rock climbing, and later, windsurfing. Every outdoor sport with any risk included at least one lesson on falling correctly.

My first rock climbing instruction, for example, began with low-level climbing practice on boulders, where the beginner risks small, manageable falls. Once I learned and practiced the basic climbing maneuvers near the ground, it was time to go higher.

In the process, I learned certain safety procedures including the proper use of ropes, anchors, and verbal commands. The latter helped ensure that all the climbers were protecting each other's safety. Before I began even my first small ascent, I learned to attach one end of a safety line (the belay line) to my harness and to check verbally with my climbing

partner, who was safely anchored and properly holding the other end of the line. The protocol ensured that the appropriate precautions had been taken and that the climbing team was in good communication before the ascent began.

As in any sport, a beginner needs to focus on the basics. Once on the rock face, balance and grip are nearly impossible to maintain for a beginner; more so if the rock face is at all challenging. Even the simplest moves might cause them to fall, so one of their first lessons should be in how to "fall safely." While this might sound like an oxymoron at first glance, you are simply foolhardy if you don't learn how to fall in a sport like rock climbing!

Practicing the fall at a low height is invaluable for all concerned, but it also affects the climber's attitude and chances of short- and long-term success. Knowing that one is safely belayed gives needed confidence and improves one's willingness to climb higher, to try new moves, and to cope with different climbing conditions.

I had a similar experience as a student of windsurfing and later an instructor of the sport. Once again, I learned the right way to fall. At low speed, the safe bet was "The Nestea Plunge," a takeoff on an old television commercial that showed the blissful beverage drinker falling backwards into a pool, flat on her back, arms and legs outstretched. As a windsurfing instructor, I would make a game out of falling off the board right away, so everyone got used to the idea and it was part of the fun.

The practical application was that this technique (and the willingness to use it) protected knees, ankles, wrists, and

elbows from being painfully jammed on a shallow lake bottom, seafloor or sleeping stingray. At higher speeds and hooked into a harness, I learned to "ride the rig" down to avoid being catapulted dangerously far from the board, getting tangled in or beaten up by the equipment, or being slung through the sail itself like a missile.

I experienced this principle again with my first coaching instructor, Rick Tamlyn, who would physically fall down in front of the class whenever he made a mistake, then get up and shout with his arms outstretched, "Tah-dah!" His memorable pratfall was a magnificent way of reminding us that mistakes are for learning.

Mistakes are necessary for developing leaders.

Anyone learning new things will make errors. Anyone who is trying hard in a role they are unfamiliar with will make mistakes. Mistakes are expected of people who are working hard, reaching for stretch goals, and taking on added responsibilities. In fact, mistakes are necessary for developing leaders.

Encouraging mistakes

As a consultant, I have even seen mistakes encouraged by executives who want to challenge their organizations to achieve great things and develop people more fully. Anthony Romanello, a county administrator, put mistake making in his written expectations of staff, saying that there should even be "spectacular failures."

What he was trying to convey was that he wanted to see people trying so hard to make improvements, that they sometimes got the cart before the horse in a big way.

All the great managers I have known, the icons of industry we have read about, our personal role models and mentors, and champions in every field of endeavor have learned their crafts through study and practice; and they reflect sincerely on what they learned from their experiences. Before starting this book, I knew intuitively that every successful manager has made mistakes along the way—tons of them. This was confirmed by every single person I interviewed, over a hundred successful managers and leaders from a number of industries and sectors of the economy.

A seminal study of this phenomenon in the business world by Michael Lombardo and Robert Eichenger at the Center for Creative Leadership discovered how most lessons of leadership are derived solely from experience. According to their work, the lessons are learned primarily through stretch assignments, start-up opportunities, changes in scope, turn-around challenges, and hardships.

Someone once said that there is a big difference between 10 years of experience and one year of experience 10 times. What is that difference? It is the ability to learn. "Part of what differentiates why some people grow in leadership roles and others don't is how they learn," said Mike Bogenschutz, a VP Plant Operations. "You can learn in a lot of different places if you expose yourself to the right people. For instance, my son is taking karate, and when I take him to class, I always bring a book but end up listening to the life

lessons from his teacher and writing down the leadership principles he talks about."

This is the mindset of an active learner, someone who takes every opportunity (even away from the workplace) to observe, reflect upon what they are seeing, and take away important lessons. The great basketball star Michael Jordon also exemplified this never-satisfied mindset. His work ethic was legendary, but a lot of high performing individuals have that. It was his *learning ethic* that made him unique, and not all of us have retained that very special skill, perhaps first demonstrated when we learned to walk.

You will need this learning ethic to succeed, and like the stumbling toddler, you will need resilience. High performers have high expectations of themselves and others. As a result, it will be tempting to overlook your successes and dwell on your mistakes.

> *"People are scared of making mistakes. They want to make a positive impression and get things done but may not know how, or they fear consequences for errors."*
>
> –Judith B. Douglas, Client Industry Executive

Even though it is frightening, give yourself permission to fail along the way, as long as you reflect on your mistakes for a short and productive time period. Set a deadline, like the end of the week, and then remember Rick's pratfall. Smile to yourself and think, "Tah-dah, I'm still human, and I'm not through learning yet!" You must find a way to keep your mistakes in perspective; not only for yourself but also for the people you supervise. They will be watching you closely to

see if mistakes really are "OK," and you will be role modeling the all-important learning mindset.

Mistakes versus misdeeds

Before we look at why new managers make the "mistakes" they do, I'd like to clear up something else about the term. High-profile executives, politicians, and errant celebrities have exacerbated the negative stigma surrounding the word "mistake," particularly those who would like to minimize the consequences of their bad or unethical decisions by reframing what they have done. As a result, the meaning of the word has been further eroded and made somewhat confusing.

For example, no matter who is in the "hot seat" for the errors, the theme of their remarks seems to follow a certain pattern. "Now that I'm caught and my deeds uncovered, let me apologize to the public for breaking the law, to my family for letting them down, to my supporters for undermining their faith in me, and to anyone else who might have taken my words out of context and been accidentally offended."

The mistake-maker is thinking, *This carefully worded statement is to reframe what I have done as a simple mistake, one that all humans are capable of making. If I am successful in doing so, people should feel sorry for me instead of holding me accountable. This will allow me to 'stand up, dust myself off' and go about my business without any real consequences.*

The transgressions that are recast as "mistakes" are actually something else entirely. Mistakes are for learning, but misdeeds are for consequences. There is a distinction here with a very big difference.

Mistakes are for learning, but misdeeds are for consequences.

"Mistakes" are understandable oversights, miscues or missteps that have short-term or minimal consequences, and they offer learning opportunities, such as these:

- Misunderstanding or misinterpreting rules or guidelines
- Miscalculating collateral impacts
- Overlooking details, making technical errors, or accidentally omitting information
- Making errors from lack of awareness, not lack of concern
- Making errors with the best intentions even though the impacts are more serious
- Using poor judgment due to inexperience
- Taking action that is misaligned with expectations or job responsibilities
- Making erroneous or naïve assumptions
- Taking action that somewhat or temporarily diminishes one's credibility
- Taking action that inadvertently leads to relatively minor consequences
- Causing harm to the organization or stakeholders that is repairable in the short term

- Making self-centered decisions that have consequences for the individual

"Misdeeds," on the other hand, are conscious decisions with avoidable, serious or long-term consequences, which are likely to derail careers. They include the following:

- Breaking the law
- Breaking a code of ethics or other explicit rules of conduct
- Ignoring warnings, a pattern of repeating the same mistakes
- Deceiving others overtly or covertly by deliberate omission
- Acting in one's own self-interest without sufficient regard for the concerns of stakeholders or the organization as a whole
- Showing egregiously poor judgment, clearly knowing better but proceeding anyway
- Performing poorly due to lack of effort
- Causing harm to the well-being or livelihood of others.
- Damaging the organization's reputation
- Taking action that has major negative consequences to the organization or its stakeholders
- Causing harm to the organization or its stakeholders that is avoidable and long term
- Making self-centered decisions that lead to negative consequences that others are forced to live with

Misdeeds can also be patterns of behavior that have serious and long-term consequences, such as the manager who creates a hostile work environment with ill-chosen humor,

lewd remarks or repeated harassment of co-workers. While misdeeds are forgivable, particularly by the charitable among us, they still have consequences.

Why do new managers make the mistakes they do?

Whatever time and resources new managers have had to devote to their education has focused mostly on learning a trade or a technical body of knowledge. They have had little if any training or experience to prepare them for a leadership role. People "go into" law, engineering, medicine or forestry. They don't "go into" leadership, per se. Alternatively, they are attracted to the mission of an organization or a cause. Once again, they are pursuing another line of work, not usually the profession of management.

While they might have taken some form of business training, they have had little education or experience in the art of leadership, which differs from management. While management education includes a few leadership classes, the emphasis in business schools is on teaching management techniques not leadership skills (i.e., master's in business administration). There are very few schools that teach a curriculum on leadership.

While management education includes a few leadership classes, the emphasis in business schools is on teaching management techniques not leadership skills.

Unless they have had some other

previous experience with leading adults in the workplace, most new managers are ill prepared for the role. Conni Morse, a Marketing Consultant, explains it this way: "Organizations wave a magic wand and 'poof' you're a manager! I don't think the management positions I've held ever provided training, except the technical kind. I received phone numbers, job descriptions and org charts, but no training for how to manage people. I had to learn that on my own."

This is particularly true after decades of downsizing and cost cutting. During this time, the traditional methods of preparing leaders for internal succession have been drastically cut from organizations' budgets. What training that could be squeezed in happened months before it had any real relevance to the new manager, and once new managers start in their positions, they have very little time to spare for personal development. "New managers are often pushed for results that they don't know how to get," said Judith B. Douglas, a Client Industry Executive.

> *"If you are an IT guy and you are moved into real estate, for instance, the organization would naturally give you functional training. But when an IT guy is moved to management, they seldom even think about sending him back to school for that."*
> –Mike McGinley, Vice President, Operations

At least in their technical roles, people have something of a road map, an owner's manual that can be learned, replicated and fine-tuned. However in management, "There is no cookbook approach, and managers don't get to practice the

skill until they get on the job," said Robbie Coleman, a Manager of Maintenance and Engineering. "Even a doctor gets to practice first! Leadership skills have to be tried out to understand more about which ones are most effective and in what situations."

It looks easier than it really is

From where they sit, most aspiring managers perceive relatively little difference between what they are currently doing and what they would be doing as a manager. If anything, it looks easier and appears to have better benefits! This would be extremely rare if ever true and the sign of a poorly designed or badly run work system. The truth is that the job is far more difficult than it appears on the surface. Karen Webb, a President & CEO, said it this way: "I once had a staff member comment that he would love to have the power and prestige of my job every day. I said, 'You'd have to take the problems, too, and you don't see those!' I don't show those; that would be a morale breaker."

Thinking the job is easy leads to mistakes because the new manager underestimates the complexity of the role, prepares less for the transition, and fails to learn fast enough to make a successful transition. "There is a big difference between knowing something intellectually and understanding something in your heart," said Robyn Bumgardner, a Human Resources Professional. "Even though they are two sides of the same coin, one doesn't substitute for the other, and one is incomplete without the other." A number of my clients have reported being "in a state of shock" for their first 12 to 18 months as a new manager. Even if they had read some books

and taken some training, the transition can be painfully difficult.

Good and bad role models

Quite naturally, people learn from what and whom they see. Without more advanced preparation, new managers will rely on the mental images in their head. "My leadership style is a 'crock pot' of other people's styles," said Joe Gilkerson, an Acting Director of Human Resources. People learn from role models, and this starts when they are children.

Our first examples of leadership come from our parents (or guardians), which can be good influencers or bad ones. The way your parents raised you will certainly have an impact on your approach to others, how you manage conflict, reward and recognize others, hold people accountable, build others' self-esteem, or tear it down. Our value systems are established early, and these are what drive our behaviors. Alarmingly, if you haven't learned certain values by the time you are six years old, you are unlikely to learn them as an adult, so your early childhood is a key component in your temperament and your management style. People who raised us were our first and most powerful role models, for better or worse.

> "Problems occur when people simply emulate what they see...they naturally assume that this is the way to do things. This perpetuates the culture of a particular organization without even meaning to do so."
> —Jim Horton, Sales Manager

As adolescents, people observe role models in the public domain and start to make choices about whom they admire

and wish to emulate. They pick up cues from members of their family, their neighbors, popular culture, and their peers. They begin comparing what they have seen inside the home with other examples and start to experiment with various identities. Because of their choices, they begin to associate with certain groups of friends, some helpful and some quite the opposite.

The process continues in the workplace, where people see a wide variety of management and leadership behaviors. Mark D. Cox, a President/CEO, was making this point when he said, "As human beings, we do a lot of emulating what we see and experience. I see many managers who try to clone themselves to a set of behaviors that they assume are the right ones. The fundamental mistake is that what you have seen and experienced may not have worked for you or anyone else. Make sure you halfway understand that."

> *"We have probably had more bad role models than good ones, but it is hard for the inexperienced to distinguish between the two."*
>
> –Trent Beck, Senior Manager

During the early phases of a career, it is not always possible to distinguish accurately between good and bad management behavior. As Bob Scudder, an Executive and Career Development Coach, put it, "People don't understand what good management is, so they emulate what they have seen and experienced. For example, I asked a brand new manager, 'What is the main distinction between the individual and supervisor role?' She said, 'Now I can tell people what to do.' That's how she saw it. So I asked, 'Then what do you

do if they don't comply?' and she said, 'Then I punish them.' Unfortunately, new managers have a lot of poor role models on which to base their actions."

Many interviewees reported having learned as much from bad bosses as good ones, but they were not yet fully equipped to discern the difference. Therefore, they think that those management behaviors must be the expectation of all leaders in their organization. As a result, they experiment with (and in some cases adopt) these behaviors for themselves.

Default to their natural tendencies

We all develop patterns of preferences based on a combination of our personality and environment. Many people in business are familiar with Carl Jung's personality theories made famous by Isabel Briggs Myers and Katharine Cook Briggs in the *Myers-Briggs Type Indicator*. In this assessment tool and accompanying workshops, people learn to self-identify their preferences in four major areas: how data are gathered, how decisions are made, how energy is gained, and how activity is structured.

Many interviewees reported having learned as much from bad bosses as good ones, but they were not yet fully equipped to discern the difference.

In advanced classes, people also learn that there is a predictable sequence in which each of the 16

"types" learn and use alternative preferences on their way to being well-rounded adults. This theory holds that we maintain the same preferences for a lifetime but that we become more adept at using all the preferences "situationally."

These preferences represent certain comfort zones, or *modus operandi* that come naturally to each of us. For example, signing one's name with the preferred hand gives the sensation of a preference. It flows easily, requires little thought, and goes quickly. Repeating this process with the non-preferred hand demonstrates what it is like to be operating outside of one's comfort zone. This alternative requires concentration, feels awkward, and takes more time.

When new managers step into their challenging new roles, they are very likely to do what comes naturally; we all would. "Individuals gravitate to their comfort zones, and many things reinforce this tendency," explained Larry Raynor, a Senior Director. "If you're analytical, you will do the most number crunching. If you're an engineer, you will take a scientific approach. If you're a people person, you'll build relationships." What comes naturally does not represent a wide-enough skill set to be successful as a manager, so managers need to know their strengths and become well balanced.

In fact, what comes naturally might be the polar opposite of what is effective. Bill Galanko, a Vice President - Law, explained it this way: "Good leadership is at least partly driven by personality, what comes naturally. However, because of their tendencies, people will look for ways not to

do what they know they need to do. For example, for an introvert, it is easy to stay in your office rather than go out and foster relationships."

Psychologist Robert Hogan also illustrates how "what comes naturally" can get a manager into trouble. In his research on executive derailment, he shows how unaware managers under stress can rely too heavily on their strengths, which may have been apparent in other jobs or organizations. Detail-oriented individuals, for example, are promoted for their diligence but can become micromanagers in a leadership capacity. Creative people may come up with so many ideas that they don't stop long enough to execute them. Fast-paced managers can lose their composure under stress, which might not have been a problem in their individual roles but can be a career-ending event in a management position.

What generally causes managers to derail, in Dr. Hogan's terms, is the over use of a preferred tendency under the following conditions: heavy workload, unusual stress, poor fit in the position, or becoming comfortable in a role and letting down one's guard. New managers quickly fall into the first two categories, putting them at immediate risk if they are not prepared.

Left alone to sink or swim
The "leadership pipeline," once a steady stream of trained and "groomed" new managers in the workplace, has slowed to a trickle. The growing shortage of prepared new managers is exacerbated by a globalized economy, the changing preferences of the workforce, exploding technologies, and

the retirement of the Baby Boom generation. Making matters even worse, the supervisors of new managers previously relied upon as first-line trainers and mentors have also had to learn their roles on the fly, and they have little time to devote to the development of their replacements.

Therefore, another reason new managers make mistakes is that they are largely left to sink or swim on their own. By the time the new manager is selected and put in position, the role is likely to have been vacant for some time, and there is a buildup of work. Immediate results are needed, and there is little room for errors or excuses. In addition, jobs change quickly in a high-tech, global, and financially insecure economy, meaning that new managers are often breaking new ground; and mentors might not have the answers. Solutions have to be found in new ways, and the new incumbent is frequently left to her own devices.

Making matters worse, today's managers of new managers are themselves new in their positions, similarly frazzled and minimally trained as coaches and mentors. They are busy keeping their own jobs and often have little time or patience to help their new managers as they would like. Also, the unprecedented layoffs and cutbacks of the last several years have put an extra burden on managers. With everyone in firefighting mode, it is little wonder that the new manager is likely to make mistakes without much of a safety net or opportunity to learn from the experience.

As a result, Sarah Gravitt-Baese, a Vice President, encourages new managers to be proactive. "Hold your manager accountable for helping you grow and develop,"

she said. "Your boss gets paid for this, so you have a right to it and will need it. If you're not getting it from them, go find someone else who will. It's that important."

In an entirely different sector, Tammi W. Ellis, an Executive Director of Organizational Development, decided at one point to take responsibility for her own development as well. "After three years of pulling out the same program memorandum and changing the date, I started stepping forward to do projects, try something new. So when a position became available, I had prepared myself more than others had. If you want to be promoted to something, act like it now," she added.

The selection process

Right behind safety, there is nothing more important to the organization than the effective hiring of its frontline managers. These decisions shape the culture of the business for better or worse, improve or degrade employee retention and morale, and lead to customer satisfaction or dissatisfaction. First-line managers are the clutch that engages the organization's engine, and they are the talent pool of its future.

Yet the process of selecting this important group of people is shortchanged every day.

First-line managers are the clutch that engages the organization's engine, and they are the talent pool of its future. Yet the process of selecting this important group of people is shortchanged every day.

Organizations put much more emphasis on how they select their technical staff and senior executives. These latter roles often incorporate psychological testing, multiple panel interviews, and/or work simulations. But new managers are often chosen "at the drop of a hat," because the candidate

- Was the best available technical expert
- Had the necessary credentials
- Was in the right place at the right time
- Had the best political and self-promotional skills
- Made the most noise about wanting the position
- Was favored by someone higher up

Perhaps the biggest assumption and enduring fallacy in the selection process, however, is that the best technical expert will be the best manager for that function. Don Sowder, a Pharmaceutical Executive, gives a good example: "A terrific sales person does not always make a terrific sales manager. This is the worst mistake that companies make, and the wrong people are promoted."

> *"Most people are just taking advantage of what comes along, whatever moves them up in the organization and without regard for their personal and professional goals or job fit."*
>
> –Bob Scudder, Executive and
> Career Development Coach

After taking part in dozens of startups, turn-around projects and expansions, I have seen smart leaders and experienced executives who know this principle to be true, still default to selecting managers with the better technical record of accomplishment. This mistake haunts them repeatedly and

sometimes dramatically when these subject-matter experts fail to mobilize their people. Furthermore, these decisions are difficult to undo without extreme embarrassment or other unsavory consequences, and the opportunity costs stay hidden for years.

Pressure to move "up or out"

After a certain point in their careers, people tend to feel they *have to* become a manager, even if they do not *want to*. For many, expectations have become so ingrained over the years that a successful career can only mean climbing the corporate ladder to the top or at least very near the pinnacle of the organization chart. A few businesses even have explicit rules that require employees to move vertically with an "up or out" philosophy. The idea of parallel career paths was conceived for this reason, to give people more than one way to grow within the same organization and to avoid forcing square pegs into round holes.

> *"Organizations create a culture of moving people up even if they are ill suited for the role. They should make it OK to continue to be a strong individual performer."*
>
> –Trent Beck, Senior Manager

As Denise G. Kasper, a Human Resources Director, noted, "The way up in most organizations is that you have to start to manage people to go higher, but you've got to want to be a manager to be a good one. Career paths need to be created for those who don't want to manage but want to progress in their technical areas."

Without such alternatives, people feel forced into jobs that are potentially a very bad fit. This is a setup for failure. While organizations do need people to move into management positions, they cannot afford leaders who do not really want the job. At best, such individuals will be slow and unenthusiastic learners. At worst, they will cause upheaval, inefficiency and turnover, undermining the work of others and clogging up the pipeline of future leaders.

"Some people are simply not cut out to be managers. No matter how hard they try, it's just not in them."
–Dave Winter, Human Resources Executive

"Being a manager is not right for everybody," explained Willis Potts, a Senior Vice President and General Manager. "It took me a while to recognize that some will be happier if they stay in an individual role. We should help people understand this. But this puts pressure on organizations to find ways for an individual contributor to have opportunity and reward without making the traditional move to management."

Titles do not matter
Don't be fooled by your job title, which might include words like supervisor, team leader, manager, foreman, chief, director, or head honcho. Titles are chosen to fit an organization's culture, an industry's heritage, or the founder's vision. They can be superlative, stuffy and even slightly demeaning, but the exact title is largely irrelevant. As long as your role involves deploying the work, monitoring the performance of others and developing the organization's talent, you are a *manager*, and that means

something very specific, which we will explore in the first chapter of this book.

You have become a technical or subject-matter expert in your chosen field, worked hard individually to achieve a significant level of success, and are now taking the leap to a management role. Like it or not, you are entering a new profession with very different skill sets, and you might not be very good at them in the beginning.

"While the best individual performers usually get promoted, they may be the least qualified," said Willis Potts. "The traits of a good manager may be diametrically opposed to what is needed in an individual job." This is not to say that high-performing individuals are less than capable of becoming good managers, but unless you at least understand that there is a big difference between the two roles, your success will be in jeopardy before you get started.

As the philosopher George Santayana once said, "Those who don't know history are destined to repeat it." My goal in writing this book is to illuminate the most common and serious mistakes that you are likely to make so that you can benefit from those who have gone before you. This is also a uniquely important turning point for you. It will establish your reputation as a leader, initiate a pattern of behaviors that will be hard to change later, and shape your trajectory to future leadership positions.

"At least the teaching profession has a body of knowledge and a licensing process," said Carol Anderson, a Chief Learning Officer. "First-time managers are often simply in the right place at the right time, getting promoted for their

individual accomplishments. Neither are they typically put through a rigorous selection process. They find it out by having to do it," she added.

Because you too will have to learn this art and science by doing it, you can still expect to make mistakes discussed in every chapter of this book. Nevertheless, by studying these common mistakes, you will

- Prevent them or mitigate their consequences
- Adapt more quickly when you recognize an error in progress
- Learn from them rather than becoming derailed by them
- Get better results from your team sooner
- Establish a solid reputation as a leader
- Attract the best talent to your team
- Have a better impact on people's lives, including your own
- Save your organization money, time, and opportunity costs

This book will also benefit more experienced managers. They will recognize some of these errors from first-hand experience, and this will help them continue to develop in those key areas. I also recommend it for the managers of new managers, because it will help them coach and mentor their subordinates at a particularly important time in their careers. In any case, this book will give you the template, language and ideas you need to help subject-matter experts become expert managers of people, sooner rather than later.

INTRODUCTION
ASSIGNMENTS FOR A SUCCESSFUL ASCENT TO MANAGEMENT

❑ Review the mistakes you made in the early stages of your current job. Discuss how you learned from them, as these are clues to your learning preferences.

❑ Interview experienced managers about the mistakes they made in their careers and how they learned from them.

❑ Find your organization's management competency model or a generic one, and build your development plan around those key success factors.

❑ Study your organization's management development system, locate the entry points, and make a plan for how you might get started early.

❑ Seek informational interviews with human resource professionals, training and development experts, and leadership coaches as you construct a development plan.

❑ Find a talented manager, mentor, or coach to help you develop your insights and skills faster than they might evolve accidentally.

❑ Volunteer for stretch assignments, internships, or temporary apprenticeship programs that give you a chance to "try on" the role at a low altitude to see if it is something you want to learn more about.

❑ Locate or develop a support group (or "mastermind" group) of like-minded people who aspire to be managers and are learning at about the same pace as you.

❑ Review the mistakes in this book and assess your willingness to make these errors as you learn on the job.

"You may have been promoted for your technical abilities but these are irrelevant to your success as a manager."

–Tom Davidson

Rockin'
With the Wrong Role
Underestimating the shift in responsibilities

At one point, my wife and I had moved 10 times in seven years. Naturally, we got tired of it, but we also learned a lot about the moving process. Before our last move, we decided to try to sell our home ourselves; making us what the industry calls a couple of "FSBOs" (for sale by owner), not a complimentary term!

We had seen what realtors do and didn't think it looked that difficult. You show a few houses, sign some papers and collect a big commission; at least that was how we saw it. We knew there was something more to it, that there were some classes and certifications, but we had also seen others sell their own houses and "keep the commission," so we tried it.

Big mistake. We wasted time, frustrated potential buyers, and opened our house to strangers in completely inappropriate ways. After a few months, we realized what a horrible mistake it was and turned things over to a professional, swearing to be "poster children" for the real estate industry one day. There is a great deal more to the process than we ever realized, and the advice they give and service they provide is worth their commission. With proper training and guidance, we might have made good real estate agents one day, but we were completely ill prepared for the role at the time.

In a similar way, managers rarely understand their new role. They witness certain parts of it, perceive only a few differences, and exaggerate the benefits. They realize at a superficial level that the job is different, but they do not (cannot) understand just how different it is.

"When I see a new manager, I think, 'By the way, congratulations, and all the skill sets you have just became obsolete.' Leading a team of people is very different than doing the work on your own, so the new job or promotion that got you to this role means you have more work to do, that you need to reinvent yourself in many ways. Leading is about working backwards from the end state that you want to create and how best to guide people through that long-term journey."

–Karl Werwath, Managing Vice President

In fact, if new managers did have the full picture, many would not venture into the profession, would stay in their

individual or technical roles, and turn the job over to someone else! Even some successful managers I interviewed had a few regrets in this regard, but most simply wished that they "knew then what they know now."

In some visible ways, the new job appears familiar and relatively easy because you will likely be operating in the same type of business, one where you probably have some expertise. "It's like you were the left rear tire expert," explained Ron Thiry, a Vice President of Operations, "but now you are responsible for the whole car." Not only that, you are now accountable for the entire assembly line, the parts inventory, the budget, the vacation schedule, the personnel problems, the price of fuel, and the weather!

While this may be exaggerating to make the point, the change in scope is surprising, even shocking. That is why some experienced managers thinking back might say, "Life would have been a lot easier if I had remained the expert of the left rear tire." Of course then, they would have missed other challenges, benefits, and rewards. It is a mixed blessing, and a career decision that should not be taken lightly, especially when you know that about 40 percent of newly appointed leaders derail, plateau, or fall short of needed goals in their first 18 months.

Far too many individuals end up in a supervisory capacity because it was simply the next rung on the "corporate ladder." They had no significant interest in being a manager, had not given it much thought, but now they are one. One day, an offer came along that had more money attached to it, and it seemed like the thing to do at the time.

As a result, the organization loses a productive individual performer and perhaps gains an unhappy and unproductive manager, possibly one who alienates staff and undermines results. More than the loss of a technically competent contributor, the organization has now caused multiple problems. Exacerbating this further, an unsatisfactory promotion is very difficult to undo, for both the individual and the organization.

This chapter will help you get a better sense of what the role will be like so that you can prepare in advance, adapt more effectively, or choose to stay in your current role as an individual contributor.

The grass is greener

How many times have you thought how nice it would be to have your own business? You might have longed for the freedom from company politics, the chance for a more lucrative future, and the ability to set your own hours. While these certainly have their benefits, what you cannot possibly see is the number of headaches that go with that freedom, the number of priorities that have to be juggled with that flexibility, or the burden of responsibility that goes with owning your own business.

> *As a result, the organization loses a productive individual performer and perhaps gains an unhappy and unproductive manager.*

Just before I entered private practice, a friend and mentor, Dave DeBaugh, said, "Until you've put your mortgage payment on a credit card, you'll never know what it's like to work for yourself." Even though he knew that it would be difficult for me to understand until I actually made the leap, he was doing his best to give me a clear picture so that I would make an informed decision. Even though his message was frightening, I was still motivated enough to continue. However, I have always been grateful to him for helping me to see what I was getting myself into, and that is why this chapter is so important.

This failure is not the fault of the new manager. It's the fault of their supervisors for not helping them understand their role.

It's hard to know the role if you haven't been introduced to it properly. This failure is not the fault of the new manager. It's the fault of their supervisors for not helping them understand their role.

Large organizations used to "groom" their future leaders by having them work in many of the jobs they would one day supervise. Unfortunately, that luxury has fallen by the wayside in most organizations through downsizing, thinned ranks of middle managers, and slashed training budgets. In addition, people do not stay with organizations as they used to, so developmental job rotations do not have the same effect or appeal, another factor making it difficult for new managers to get a clear understanding of their new role.

Your understanding of the role is likely to be distorted if you are a high performer, consistently achieve exceptional results, or are frequently called upon for your subject matter expertise. If this is the case, your manager has probably spent relatively less time with you than others, leaving you to do your work with little interference, mostly providing support only when necessary. As a result, you may not have witnessed many of the problems that he/she has had to contend with, many of them related to underperformers, organizational politics, or being held accountable for the work of others.

In addition, your manager has probably been acting as a buffer for you, so that you could concentrate on your "left rear tire" job and not be burdened with unnecessary headaches and distractions of the entire car. Your supervisor has been doing you a favor, but now you are entering their world, and you will not be protected anymore. Now you must become the buffer for others, the resource provider, and the problem solver.

I have had the privilege of working with hundreds of aspiring managers as they go through management assessment and development centers, which place them in realistic simulations of a manager's job. These include workplace coaching scenarios, group decision-making activities, and administrative challenges. One of the universal comments I hear from these future leaders is how it was "eye opening" and "humbling." It is not uncommon to hear that someone would "never look at his manager the same way again," having gained a real appreciation for what they deal with "behind the scenes." The participants are

frequently taken aback when they discover how "uncooperative" or "emotional" subordinates can become if situations are not deftly handled.

Participants are vexed by the complexity of problems, the number of people with "issues," and the constant problem of competing priorities. No longer is it sufficient to please your one and only boss. For your boss to be "pleased" now, you have to satisfy a wider array of needs, including those of your team, customers, peers, and publics. Very often, the assessment experience itself changes the new manager's perspective. Countless participants have said, "I came in thinking like a (sales) rep and left thinking like a manager."

"Some people have a misperception of what the role really is, and you can't really understand it until you are in it," said Robyn Bumgardner. "It's like when a parent says 'This is going to hurt me more than it's going to hurt you'; we really don't get it until we are a parent ourselves," she concluded.

Over the septic tank
Erma Bombeck once wrote, "The grass is always greener over the septic tank." Her analogy helps illustrate that the benefits of being a manager come with some tough (some would call "dirty") jobs, which is also to point out that the role is not for everyone.

I once had a boss who knew that I wanted to be a manager someday, and like any good manager himself, he took various opportunities to teach me the lessons I would need. One day, he let me know of some downsizings that would be announced very shortly, and he wanted me to take part in the firing of an employee–a friend of mine. The event itself was

traumatic for me. By the time it was over, I was an emotional wreck, worse off than the man being let go. That one single experience prepared me in a number of important ways, because I eventually had to fire people myself.

When I have told this story in seminars, people have questioned my boss' actions, wondering if the lesson might have "backfired" or discouraged me from being a manager. It might have, but I think he was doing the organization and me a big favor. While it gave me pause, it did not dissuade me from my goal. More than anything, it helped me to make a clear-headed decision, not a haphazard one, about my decision to move into leadership positions.

"Really question if you want to be a doer or a leader of people. Ask yourself whether you really understand what you are taking on here. It's kind of like a marriage. You have to be committed to it. You take responsibility for what other people do and how they do it. You have to be willing to give good and bad news, and you have to be accountable when things go wrong," explained Donna Blatecky, a Deputy Director in government service.

What the role is like

Because the role is hard to describe in words alone, descriptions are sometimes reduced to textbook-type language. I believe that is why a number of my interviewees offered analogies and metaphors to help convey the more complex picture and what the role is really like.

Anthony Romanello recalled the following canoe analogy: "Becoming a manager is like moving from the front seat to

the rear. The job in the front seat is to paddle hard to propel the boat. The guy in the back does his share of paddling but his fundamental purpose is steering. If both canoeists are paddling hard (in other words, there is no manager) then they are moving fast but aimlessly."

If you have ever been whitewater canoeing with more than one person, you know how critical both functions can be (and how frustrating it is if there is a lack of coordination or communication). The person in the front can also do some steering, but it is a special kind of maneuver ("the draw stroke") that finely tunes the direction of the canoe so that the bow misses rocks, often at the last possible moment! It is a much more localized maneuver that can save the boat from capsizing.

There are other strokes specific to each position in the boat, and when they are coordinated, a canoe can be guided successfully through very rough water. When they are uncoordinated, a canoe can be turned over on the calmest river. I accidentally dumped my friend and myself in the smooth water of Virginia's Pamunkey River when I foolishly tried to demonstrate what "could happen."

While you may have been a terrific paddler at the front of the boat, it doesn't mean you'll excel in the rear seat. "The difference is between doing and orchestrating the work of others, organizing and guiding its execution. The mistake new managers make here is not realizing the difference between the two," explained Robyn Bumgardner.

It is not copping out to keep your hands off the controls and let others have them. If you are an accountant, it is not lazy

that you do not personally close the books anymore and that you let others handle what you used to do yourself. If you are a fire fighter, you are not above getting your hands dirty if you don't grab a water hose, don an air pack, and enter the burning building with your people. Your job is to make sure that they know how to do those jobs, have the resources they need, and help coordinate their work so they are safe and successful.

> *"As a manager, I am first and foremost a servant. I am never allowed to carry the ball. My job is to block so you have the goal line. I clear the way for you to do your job. It is a mindset that the managers should provide resources, encourage the heart and remove barriers."*
> –Willis Potts, Vice President and General Manager

On another level, your role becomes even more difficult to describe but no less important. This is also where the great managers excel and the poor ones languish. "It's all about setting the tone for the organization, all the way from the chairman to the first-line leader," said Willis Potts. "The role of the leader is to create the environment necessary to accomplish goals," added Mark D. Cox. While the CEO is busy trying to influence the culture of the entire organization, you have the same responsibility to your work unit, no matter how big or small it might be. You already are influencing the tone of the work environment, so you might as well shape it in a positive and productive manner.

As a leadership consultant to a range of organizations, I can tell a lot about the team's culture by the way people talk to

one another, the questions they ask, their tone of voice, the problems they are having, the appearance of their workplaces, what's on the bulletin boards, and even the pictures on the walls. An organization's culture is a collection of norms and behaviors that arise among its members, and one can find many different cultures within the same organization. These can be traced directly to the leader of that work unit.

> *"Assume that people are trying to do the right thing that some condition is getting in their way if they are not. Remove the barriers and the right things will happen; people will rise to the occasion."*
> –Jim Horton, Sales Manager

Karl Werwath, a Managing Vice President, illuminates the role this way: "The shift to management is like the difference between being a hunter and being a farmer. The hunter goes out with a maniacal focus on delivering short-term results, putting meat on the table. The farmer has a longer-term focus, not only planting the seeds but also preparing the ground and nourishing the garden over time. You can't force the flower to bloom, but you can make conditions right so that it will." While immediate results will always be needed at every level, the new manager has a harder time taking this longer view.

Management vs. Leadership
A discussion on this topic usually invites debate about the difference between "management" and "leadership." My premise is that if you are responsible for the productivity and well-being of others, then you are a manager no matter what

title you were assigned. As a result, your job has three parts: subject matter expertise (i.e., technical and business knowledge), coordinating resources (i.e., administration), and galvanizing people (i.e. leadership) to get results. It is a classic three-legged stool analogy, requiring the incumbent to manage things and to lead people to accomplish needed goals. Without any one of the three legs, the stool falls over, and the manager fails.

"You have to learn and understand the people side of the business, not just your technology."
—Tom Mettlach, Operations Manager

While most new managers have sound technical knowledge in their field and know something about coordinating resources, they know much less about leading people. For many organizations, there is almost no testing or evaluation of leadership potential, either because they don't know how to measure this or don't value it sufficiently in their managers. In more sophisticated organizations, new manager candidates have likely shown some evidence of leadership (i.e., taken initiative), even if they have not had formal leadership responsibilities per se. Nevertheless, it is one thing to "show leadership" and quite another to "be an effective leader."

It is one thing to "show leadership" and quite another to "be an effective leader."

While there is some overlap, the difference between management and leadership is significant enough that one can be a good manager and a poor leader, a poor manager and a good leader, both, or neither. As illustrated in the list of functions below, the management role tends to involve gathering objective data, planning, allocating, and decision-making. The leadership functions are most often related to people, human interaction, understanding organization behaviors, and mobilizing individuals or teams.

Ken Allen, a Non-profit Executive Director, said, "The job of a manager is to coordinate the organization's activities towards a common vision and allocate resources among competing priorities. This requires an understanding of the organization's mission, priorities, and available assets. It is not unlike trying to solve a *Rubik's Cube*. As a new manager, I learned that getting all the pieces to match is harder than it appears." Some major *management* functions include the following:

- Planning and scheduling
- Budgeting dollars
- Allocating scarce resources
- Monitoring quality
- Meeting company standards
- Measuring results
- Improving processes
- Finding efficiencies
- Managing time
- Solving problems
- Minimizing risks
- Protecting health and safety

- Meeting regulatory requirements
- Controlling costs
- Purchasing and negotiating
- Delegating and monitoring work
- Forecasting output, data, and resources

Mark D. Cox introduces the concept of leadership this way: "The days of hierarchy are dead. The fundamental shift is to more of the leadership attributes and less of the management ones, but these take time to develop. We still have way too much emphasis on managing and monitoring tasks versus facilitating, mentoring and building the resource to accomplish goals." Some of the major *leadership* functions include these:

- Creating a shared vision
- Setting direction
- Inspiring people
- Developing the work environment
- Building teams and teamwork
- Facilitating group dynamics
- Initiating and managing change
- Selecting and developing talent
- Modeling the way
- Encouraging and rewarding
- Removing barriers
- Advocating for the organization
- Catalyzing creativity
- Removing barriers
- Enhancing communications
- Confronting performance problems
- Taking accountability and responsibility

- Challenging the status quo
- Identifying and mobilizing diverse stakeholders

> *"The most visionary leader I knew was not a good manager. His tendency was to kill people who weren't getting on the boat with his vision. But his vision counted for nothing if it couldn't be translated and put into practice. Instead, he pushed, and dead bodies were everywhere. What was he going to do about his vision when everyone was dead? It was an epiphany for me as well. Vision is one thing but the way you make it come alive is another. Once he realized this, he was able to enlist the support needed to bring his vision to fruition with an army of support."*
> –Judith B. Douglas, Client Industry Executive

Strategic vs. Tactical

New managers need to gain altitude in their perspective. "They don't have a concept for how the whole organization fits together, how the processes connect. Typically, they have worked only in their small functional area of the business," explained Bob Scudder. It takes some time, but the sooner you start thinking "big picture," the better. This means seeing how different parts of the business are interconnected, thinking laterally outside of your immediate area of concern, and planning and taking action for the long term, generally six months to two years into the future at this level. The higher you rise in an organization, the farther ahead you should be thinking and acting.

Seeing "linkages" refers to the ability to perceive patterns and to make logical deductions about them. For example, a new bank manager should be able to detect a change in customer behavior and how that is connected to the bank's marketing methods. A new construction manager needs to monitor the quality of results and determine if a change is related to faulty material or human error. A new sales manager has to detect complaints and rumors among the workforce or among customers to perceive a threat or deduce an opportunity.

The higher you rise in an organization, the farther ahead you should be thinking and acting.

In addition, the new manager has to start thinking "laterally," outside the confines of her local department, functional group or geographic region. Without proper regard for the tangential impact of your decisions, a novice manager might inadvertently cause problems elsewhere. As an individual contributor, you could let the "chips fall where they may." As a manager, you take on responsibility for both the intended and the unintended consequences.

Inter-departmental conflict is a good example of this. Marketing sometimes develops new messages and materials without consulting sales, and as a result, the products are less than helpful and go unused, wasted. The sales department sometimes promotes products with a certain bonus rate to the sales professionals but they cannot be manufactured in sufficient quantity or to the given specifications by the

production department. In these cases, people may have felt as though they were just doing their jobs, but somewhere in these examples, the managers were not doing theirs.

> *"You may have great people skills but not be an effective leader. Without vision and goals, how in the world do you make progress? Folks miss the skill set of goal setting and tracking to them because they get caught up in the day-to-day hustle."*
>
> —Tom Mettlach, Operations Manager

As an individual performer, you are likely to have focused on daily, weekly or monthly goals. Perhaps as a sales representative, you needed to make an average number of calls per week. An attorney might be measured on billable hours per day, a week or a month. An accountant may have to complete a required number of audits or tax returns in a given period. As a manager, you will certainly be concerned about these metrics, but you must add the timeframes of quarters and years to your metrics and goals.

> *"Rather than step back and think strategically about what needs to get done, I would be in firefighting mode more than I should. It's a crutch to do whatever comes up that day."*
>
> —Bill Galanko, Vice President - Law

In addition, your goals will change from basic and easily measured targets to more qualitative and difficult to reach. Your additional new objectives will have to do with making system improvements. You are likely to be more concerned with cross-departmental projects, selecting and installing new products or technologies, and mobilizing diverse teams

from various disciplines to accomplish a groundbreaking objective. During all of this, you will still be accountable for short-term results.

It has been said, "It's hard to be strategic when your hair is on fire." As a new manager, your hair will be on fire a lot with the tactical demands of the day-to-day. However, this will not absolve you from the lateral and long-term needs of the business.

> *"The leader's job is to be more of a strategist; manager's is one of getting the work done. The overlap between the two is that you need to be thinking forward while doing what you have to do today."*
> —Denise G. Kasper, Human Resources Director

Multiple stakeholders
A stakeholder is anyone who has a substantial interest in your part of the business, and that may be a lot more people than you may realize. For example, as an individual sales professional, your stakeholders consist primarily of your customers and your boss. As soon as you become a district sales manager, the list of people who want something from you grows dramatically. In this case, that would include not only your boss but also your boss's bosses and a whole host of customers, vendors, and other publics, not to mention your subordinates.

As an individual contributor, your efforts were undoubtedly appreciated, but they had relatively little overall impact on the business compared to that of your new job, and your

bosses know this. Because you are responsible for larger decisions and for leading people, more layers of management will be interested in what you do and how you do it. As a result, you will now appear on the radar screen several layers up, possibly as high as the vice president or CEO-level depending upon the size and nature of the organization and your work.

These added layers of management who have an interest in what's going on in your area are all stakeholders too, and it is unlikely that they will funnel everything neatly through your supervisor as the organization chart implies. Even if they do not contact you directly, they are paying attention to what happens in your area, and you can be sure they are talking to your bosses about you.

For instance, as a public affairs officer for a large paper mill, it was not unusual for me to get phone calls directly from the Chairman of the Board, many layers of management above my pay grade. I learned that if he was interested in what I was doing, then everybody between him and me was interested in what I was doing and how I was doing it. These people became my stakeholders as well.

Because you are a decision-maker and have positional authority in the organization as a new manager, many people outside your business will also expect some of your time and attention. These are also stakeholders, even potential associates and bosses. Many of them will also be important to you because they will be supplying you with needed information, products or services that are relevant to your

productivity or the efficiency of your team. They cannot be ignored and might rank as a very high priority.

> *"You can't be afraid to take calculated risks. But you have to have political sense, too; if you're a new manager, you're not going to win the battle with a VP. What's needed is managerial courage and political savvy."*
>
> –Larry Raynor, Senior Director

As a new manager in the manufacturing sector, you may now have to meet with chemical suppliers, parts distributors, or waste disposal representatives. They can also help or hurt your business, so these are valuable partnerships to develop and maintain. Furthermore, these tangential relationships can be even more difficult to develop and maintain because you have little or no real authority over them. Your human relations, negotiation and partnering skills will be tested daily with these individuals and groups.

If you are a perfectionist, you may be in trouble as a manager. Your drive for quality is commendable and probably contributed to your success thus far, but this tendency can also be your downfall.

You will now have additional customer stakeholders, both internal and external. Sometimes they will want and need direct access to you, even though your subordinates primarily should attend to them. You may need to help build or repair relationships, investigate problems for

yourself, or at least be responsive when customers contact you directly.

Furthermore, the general public will now consider you part of the management team of your organization, so what you do or how you behave on the outside of the entity becomes a reflection on the business itself. Like it or not, you will be scrutinized 24 hours a day by people who associate you with your organization.

Willis Potts knew this point quite well. "I always sat my new supervisors down and made a speech that 'you represent me and the company 24 hours a day. They look to you, know who you are, and you can't separate your life into pieces. You are the same person away from the job as on the job.' I expected them to abide by certain values both inside and outside the workplace. It was part of their building trust in their people, so hiring the right person was extremely important to me at this level," he said.

On any given day, you or your part of the business might be the subject of a news story, thus making the media your stakeholder at all times. No matter what business you are in, you will have special interest groups who want to follow your activities or launch a campaign. The public gives you permission to operate your business. Depending upon your industry, you may also have one or more union organizations very much interested in your treatment of employees, the integrity of your communications, and virtually every personnel decision you make.

The new manager needs to be aware of this change in scope of visibility, be initially prepared to juggle the multiple

demands on her time, and extract herself from the daily fire-fighting mode long enough to deal with these important stakeholders effectively. It is a difficult and daunting challenge. The simple solution at the individual-contributor level has been to simply do what your boss asks of you and let others deal with the fallout. Your boss set the priorities before. Now you have to decide relative urgencies and get things moving.

Never enough of anything
As a manager, you will never have enough time, resources or information. Your world is about to go from "black and white" to totally "gray." Staying up late and working all weekend will never enable you to catch up. That special project will not get your full attention. You will never have the "whole story."

If you are a perfectionist, you may be in trouble as a manager. Your drive for quality is commendable and probably contributed to your success thus far, but this tendency can also be your downfall. Charlie Finley, a Non-profit Association Manager, told this relevant story: "Long ago, before I knew what he meant, my father would tell me, 'the world has little use or need for perfectionists.' This is not to be confused with failing to strive to do your best. Too often

Your definition of a "good decision" has to change. As a perfectionist, you probably believe that the only successful decision is the correct one.

48

perfection leads to inaction or failure to make a decision."

As a manager you will always wish that you had more information or the right information to make your decisions easy and consistently correct. Very often the information you have will be partial, third hand, or conflicting with other data. Since you cannot be everywhere at once, you will need to piece together 80 percent of what you need and be willing to make decisions based on that.

Your definition of a "good decision" has to change. As a perfectionist, you probably believe that the only successful decision is the correct one. As a manager, you will come to think of a quality decision as one that

- Uses the group's resources wisely
- Is made in a timely manner
- Is high quality based on the information at hand
- Generates a strong commitment for implementation

Accountability and recognition

I was responsible for wood procurement in a large territory including rail yards, truck yards and wood dealer operations in central Virginia. One day I got a call that an employee had been injured on one of my wood yards. Thankfully, it was not a serious injury. He had gotten his hand caught in the scale house door, as it slammed shut. With all the heavy equipment in operation, my first thought was one of relief, that it could have been a lot worse.

However, my boss was furious and held me personally responsible for the man's stitches. How could I have let this happen? What kind of an operation was I running? Don't

people know how to act so that they will be safe at all times? How was I going to prevent this from ever happening again? These were questions of accountability, the *ability* to answer for, explain, and rectify problems.

I truly believed that there was nothing I could have done to prevent the accident; after all, I was a hundred miles away at the time! I was stunned to find out just how deep my responsibility truly ran for everyone's safety. After all the training and pep talks, it had just not sunk in until that day. Safety was the highest priority, and I had not done enough to prevent this accident. This meant I had not done enough to prevent larger accidents either. That would change, and I never forgot the lesson.

As the manager, you are now accountable for everything that happens in your area of responsibility. While that sounds obvious, it has important ramifications for how you do your job. You can't do everything, be everywhere, and make all the decisions. Yet you're still *responsible* for everything. Thus, you need to build a work system in which people are clear about expectations, have a real sense of ownership, know what to do and be willing to do it well, even when you're not around.

Something else to which you will not be accustomed will be the lack of recognition and appreciation for your hard work. This is especially so if you were in an organization that heaped adulation on individual achievers. Do not expect this as a manager. Your last job might have been all about you, but this one is all about them. If you try to make it about you, your team will detect this at once and abandon you.

"As a manager, don't always expect praise. A lot of times we do a good job and get no feedback, but you can expect plenty when things are not up to par, even if you're doing a great job," said Kathy Stover, an Assistant Vice President of Clinical R&D. As a result, the bulk of your reward and recognition will have to come from within you, which is one of the reasons this job is not for everyone.

New roles and responsibilities

In 1993, basketball great Charles Barkley was confronted about his unseemly off-the-court behavior, including on- and off-court fights. He was asked, "What kind of role model are you? Don't you see how your behavior is impressing young people in a negative way?"

He responded by insisting that he was *not* a role model and that "a million guys can dunk a basketball in jail," further asking if *they* should be role models. He was saying that "role model" was not his job. He did not accept it, and it was not fair to hang it on him.

While Barkley's perspective is understandable and he is certainly not alone in his beliefs, he was either missing or rejecting an important point. Barkley could not change the fact that he was affecting people's lives, positively or negatively. These were the unintended consequences, whether he took responsibility for them or not. He was a role model, whether he liked it or not.

In a similar way, managers affect people's lives, whether or not they realize it, want it, or embrace that responsibility. For example, managers shape the quality of life at work for their employees, the safety and well-being of their

subordinates, the level of people's skills and proficiencies, the frequency and quality of learning opportunities, the type and amount of recognition, the helpfulness and quality of feedback, and the personnel decisions that determine pay, benefits and career trajectory.

As a manager, these responsibilities automatically become part of your job, whether you know it or not, whether you care or not, and whether you accept the responsibility or not. If you are just taking the job to check a box, climb a corporate ladder, or make more money, at least take your responsibility seriously and do your best to have a positive impact while you are in the role. If you are taking the job because you want to help people, then you can look forward to the following:

- Creating a positive work environment so that people enjoy their work and are pleased to do their best
- Teaching people how to do their jobs even better so that they have the best chance for job security, enhance their skills for future employment, and maximize their pay and benefits
- Coaching and supporting people so that they can achieve their fullest potential, reach their personal goals, and maximize their job satisfaction
- Exposing people to new experiences, challenging assignments, and career alternatives so that subordinates can explore and consider new career paths if they choose
- Giving people visibility inside and outside the organization so that as their talents and accomplishments are recognized they become known to others who might also help their career in some way

- Mentoring people whom you think would make good managers so that they advance more quickly and so the organization has sufficient talent in the pipeline for its future and on-going success

If these possibilities interest and excite you, then this role may be for you. On the other hand, if you reject the idea of being a role model and if this list sounds naive and idealistic, the role is probably not a good choice for you, at least not at this point in your career.

People problems

It is certainly true that a management role can be rewarding, even fun, but what else is under the "green grass" referred to earlier? To begin with, it is stress, ambiguity and long hours. It is juggling high priorities, multiple bosses and surprising stakeholders. You will not be able to please everyone, will get very little praise, and will receive plenty of "constructive" feedback. One day, you will sit down to do the math and wonder if that initial pay raise really compensated for the additional aggravation.

Prior to this role, the only person you had to look out for was yourself. However, in your new capacity, you will have to cope with human challenges that you did not learn about in school. This will involve everything from letting someone vent about something that just happened in their personal life, to ending their career with your organization.

Dealing with chronic performance problems will be unfamiliar work to you as well. As a superstar in your "former life," you might have known people who took a good deal of your manager's time, but you did not have to

deal with them directly. Now you do not have the luxury of letting someone else deal with it. It's no longer someone else's problem; it's yours. The very skills that got you recognition as a superior performer are not the same sets of skills that will bring you success as a manager of people.

Firing people should be a very rare occurrence, but it is sometimes part of the new role. However, it is naïve to think that you can just fire people who are underperforming. If you do this, you will be constantly filling vacancies and getting even worse overall results. Performance problems often stem from something else anyway, which you have to determine and solve. You will need to deliver other bad news as well, and you are unlikely to be prepared for any of it.

The erroneous assumption you are making is that you were promoted for having expertise in your field and that it is your technical capability that is being sought at the next level.

Putting down your tools

Having grown up in a manufacturing environment, I often heard the expression "putting down your tools" to describe the transition from technical expert to supervisor, foreman, or crew chief. If you are considering a promotion to management, the odds are high that you were good at your craft, probably even great. Furthermore, you must have liked your work, or you would not have been so good at it. As a result, you will have a

strong desire to keep your hands directly on some important parts of the work.

The assumption you're making is that you were promoted for having expertise in your field and that it is your technical capability that is needed at the next level. As logical as that sounds, *it's dead wrong*. Your technical ability means that you understand some aspect of the business that will inform your judgment, and it will give you needed credibility with your stakeholders. But it's not your job. As Denise G. Kasper put it, "Managers have to have a broader set of skills than just functional ones. In business today, you may be managing people who have more technical expertise in your functional area than you do. You don't have to be the best accountant to be an effective manager."

It will be tempting for you to keep turning all the wrenches, calling your old customers or checking the debits and credits at the close of business. It's simple, tempting and quite wrong to fall back on your technical skills. If you do, you'll be performing someone else's job and not doing yours, a double hit to the organization and an anchor on your future.

> *"You don't want to fail. So therefore you do that which requires immediate attention because that's what other people see. Often they don't see the long term plan; however, it is necessary to do both and not neglect long-term planning."*
> –Hattie D. Webb, Ed.D., School Division
> Central Office Leadership Team

"People often don't realize that when they move into a management position within their organization, their role

changes. The move from peer to manager changes your relationship with your coworkers and also changes the nature of your responsibilities. Adapting to these changes can be hard for both the manager and the others in the organization," explained Ken Allen.

You will not be the only one making this assumption. Hiring managers fall into this trap on a regular basis and at a critical time. Consciously or unconsciously, they mistakenly equate technical acumen with leadership ability. Thus, they promote their best sales professionals to be sales managers, their best machine tenders to be production managers, and their best programmers to be technology managers.

Being the best technician, however, is not a predictor of success in a management position. In fact, it can have a negative correlation. While your expertise will help you understand the business and earn initial credibility, it is not what you will need the most. In fact, it will get in the way of your success if you let it.

It's your management skills and leadership potential that should earn the position. Perhaps you have shown good people skills, initiated a process improvement, or led a successful task force of your peers. Maybe you held public office outside of work, ran the local Boy Scout troop, or were president of your civic association.

While technical results are a prerequisite, there should also be a pattern of leadership behaviors that put you on someone's radar for a promotion. As you climb even higher

in the organization your technical skills will become less and less relevant to your success, and that starts now.

Of course, you'll need to help your subordinates learn your old craft, and they may not be as good as you were, at least not right away. But they can't learn the skills they need if you do their jobs for them. They have to learn as you did, which means that someone provided the resources, training, coaching, mentoring and the opportunity to learn from their mistakes. Now, that someone is going to be you.

"I learned an important lesson about my job – by accident. It was when I was managing several hundred employees at a paper mill. I had done some things early on that alienated everyone. What changed me was an event where they took my boss and all my supervisors to work on a paper machine rebuild, leaving me and one other guy to manage our machine with no experienced supervisors. The solution, which I thought was insane at the time, was to bring in a bunch of supervisors from the office who had never worked on a paper machine in their lives to run the place for six months during the rebuild of the other machine. I met with these guys and said, 'Look, we only have one chance here, and that is for you to maintain housekeeping issues and watch out for everyone's safety, but in terms of running the paper machine, the daily decisions will be made by the machine operators, not you.' After a few months of adjustment, we set new production records for three consecutive months. It was not something I would have predicted. There was no other way to do it at the

time, but it taught me that there is a much better way to lead."

> –Jim Horton, Sales Manager

Look before you leap to leadership

There is still one more thing you need to know about the role before you sign on the dotted line. Once you move from an individual role to a management role, it becomes psychologically, politically, and sometimes financially very difficult to go back. If you find out later that the role is not for you and wish to step down, your old role is likely to have been filled and investments will have been made in your progression. You will feel the pressure of expectations from your family, your supervisors, your peers, and yourself. It will seem like you failed.

"You really need to go into situations with your eyes wide open. It's incredibly difficult to go back once you become a manager."

> –Tom Chalkley, Management Consultant

You can hope for a lateral transfer but this is rarely a good solution if you remain in a management capacity to any degree and found it to be a poor fit for you. Your reputation will be affected. The organization will consider you a risky candidate for another transfer. So look before you leap to a leadership position.

You can leave the organization, but you will have to explain your desire to return to an individual role. Other employers will be suspect of this change in direction, and they are likely to have alternative candidates without this "red flag."

Now that downsizing has touched virtually every part of the economy, there is much less stigma attached to losing one's position, but a voluntary demotion is somewhat different. The expectation remains that one who steps up to management will continue on this path, at least to some extent. This should be reason enough to think long and hard about making the move in the first place.

Remember the story about the discoverer Hernán Cortés after he landed in Mexico in 1519. He burned and grounded his ships to prevent his crews from returning to Cuba and to motivate them to succeed in the new world. You are about to enter a new world, too. For much the same reason, you better get to know your new job and prepare to step into it fully. Accept that managerial job and your ships will be burned for you. It will be difficult to go back.

MISTAKE #1
ASSIGNMENTS FOR A SUCCESSFUL ASCENT TO MANAGEMENT

❑ Ask current managers in your organization how they misunderstood or underestimated their first management position and subsequent ones. Compare their answers to the findings in this chapter.

❑ Find out as soon as possible, what is expected of you, the organization's strategy, your boss' goals, and how they should be achieved. Ask this repeatedly over time to ensure that you and your team are in synch with your supervisor and senior leadership.

❑ Build relationships with peer managers who have more experience than you do. Contact them regularly to share your challenges and get advice.

❑ Research your organization to understand how the many parts fit together. Describe the informal relationships as well as the formal ones (i.e., solid- versus dotted-line relationships).

❑ List the stakeholders who will have an interest in your role and responsibilities as a new manager (both inside and outside the organization), and develop a "mind map" that illustrates their various needs and dependencies.

❑ Find a mentor, other than your manager, who will meet with you periodically to discuss challenges you are facing, share their experience, and help you navigate the politics of your business.

❑ Research and draft a position paper on "positive politics" in the workplace, and discuss this with a senior manager.

"To be successful as a leader, your focus has to be on the achievement of others, not on your own."
–Tom Davidson

MISTAKE #2

Riding Like the
Lone Ranger

Focusing on individual accomplishment

The strong, independent and heroic persona is a powerful icon in Western cultures. Whether taken from classic literature, comic books, movies or real life, our vision of this often mythical person seems to endure across the generations. If you're like me, you can recall one or more of these characters from your youth, when they made the strongest impressions, and perhaps you still revere their ideals as adults.

Depending upon your generation, you might think of The Lone Ranger, John Wayne, Wyatt Earp, Daniel Boone, Superman, Batman, Wonder Woman, the Bionic Man, Lara Croft, Spiderman, Indiana Jones, Jack Bauer, or various

Clint Eastwood characters. Such icons are often individualistic in nature, basing their behavior on clear inner values and heroic individual action. They are stoic loners, people of few words but lots of action, and they get the job done. In all likelihood, your favorite ones save lives, sacrifice themselves when necessary, and use super skills we tend to admire. These bigger-than-life characters are respected, remembered, and—in real life—promoted!

Super Heroes and Teams

Much ado has been made about the importance of teams, teamwork, and team leadership in the last quarter century. Because organizations need both great individual performers and good team leaders they send mixed signals about what they want. As a result, many businesses still rate and rank associates based on their individual performance, install individual pay-for-performance systems, and give out lucrative individual bonuses to recognize and reward the top performers. We compliment them in front of large audiences, call them up on stage to give them awards, send them on exotic trips, put their names on plaques, and write about them in the company newsletter.

Yet individual recognition programs have shifted somewhat in the last quarter century and not only at work. From first grade through graduate school, students now generate reports and work on projects in teams. Youth sports programs now de-emphasize the individual contributor by rewarding everyone on the team, sometimes just for showing up to play! In the workplace, operating units are more often organized into teams, pods, and task forces. Titles have even changed to foster the changeover, from "supervisor" to

"team leader." Also, management "competency models," which are codified workplace behavior descriptions, now include categories like "team player" and "teambuilding."

Nevertheless, when it's time to promote someone from individual contributor to first-line manager, you can bet that one of the first criteria that will be used (and sometimes the only one) will be their level of individual performance. That's why the ranks of new managers are full of these "Lone Rangers."

The fact that individual performers get great individual results through extraordinary skill and effort is not the problem, per se. The mistake presented in this chapter tends to happen when star contributors are promoted to supervisor, and they don't shift gears. Unless they can also perform more like a super leader, then their super powers can become super problems. This chapter will report a few of the most common manifestations.

Looking Both Ways

One of the principles you probably learned as a champion performer was to please your boss. You surely did this in a number of ways, or you wouldn't be looked upon very favorably for a leadership position. Odds are good that you were responsive to her requests, focused on her goals, and made her look good to her superiors. If she said, "Jump," you

Unless they can also perform more like a super leader, then their super powers can become super problems.

asked, "How high?" If she had a problem, it became your problem. She was your number one customer. When you prioritized your work, you tuned in to her priorities, and that was just about all you needed to know.

Now that you are a manager yourself, you still have a boss that needs to be similarly respected. But it just got a lot more complicated. Your new focus has to be split between the needs of your boss, and the needs of your team. Satisfying one set of needs without attending to the other will lead ultimately to a suboptimal result.

"Unfortunately, new managers try to impress the boss rather than trying to impress their team. We don't learn the team part soon enough."

–Bob Scudder, Executive and
Career Development Coach

Before now, you were responsible for your own results. If other people floundered, got in hot water or came up short on their goals, these were not your problems. While you might have been concerned for them and maybe even responded to requests for help, it was unlikely that you got too distracted from your own responsibilities to solve their problems. After all, you were busy taking care of your business, and that was your first priority. Those problems were really your boss's concern. Well, now they are yours.

Your new role has put you squarely in the middle, between your subordinates and your boss. The bar just got raised on what will "please" your boss. You are no longer measured on individual performance. Your success is now a function

of *their* success, so the days of being the Lone Ranger are over. Instead of wearing a pair of single-focus glasses, you need to start wearing bifocals, with one lens on your boss and the other on your team.

> *"New managers can become too political with their superiors rather than learning how to manage their teams. Right away I wanted to keep my boss happy to get the next promotion and immediately lost sight of my current role. A major part of the District Manager's role is to advocate for your people to higher management. He is the buffer. The other part of the role is that he is the company's representative to his people. As a result, you walk a fine line."*
>
> –Don Sowder, Pharmaceutical Executive

The Brave New Workplace

Once upon a time, workers were fiercely loyal to their employers because jobs were scarce, and they were grateful for the work opportunity. Organizations fostered this relationship by rewarding longevity and providing extensive benefits. Decades ago, employees worked in one place for many years, hoped to spend their entire careers with one employer, and strove for the venerable "gold watch" that symbolized a long and stable occupation.

In those days, people progressed slowly but surely up the "corporate ladder." As a result, employees and employers developed certain expectations of one another. Believe it or not, if the employee remained productive, dependable, and loyal, then the employer might very well keep them

gainfully employed for a lifetime. It was a benevolent but impossible paradigm to sustain.

Starting in the late 1970s, this psychological "employment contract" began to deteriorate, and now there is little of it left. The world economy had changed; competition had exploded; technology had become king; and the costs of retaining employees (i.e., benefits, healthcare and retirement) has hit the bottom line -- hard. Investors and Wall Street analysts started to reward organizations that "reengineered" their businesses.

The era of "downsizing" had begun, and even the most loyal and long-term workers were laid off in the name of more profitable quarterly earnings reports. By the turn of the century, no sector of the economy was safe from the turbulence. Shocked employees found themselves on the street with an uncertain future, disillusioned about their former employers, and skeptical about future ones. The workplace would never be the same again.

Young people witnessed the gut-wrenching impacts on their parents and grandparents and learned a lasting lesson. As a result, the next two generations to enter the workforce (Generation-X and the Millenials) would have an entirely different outlook on the employer-employee relationship. The new norm would be much more detached, pragmatic, and self-centered and for good reason.

First, they would never be dependent on a single employer. Job-hopping would go from being a frowned upon to being acceptable and encouraged practice. Second, they would be

as self-sufficient as possible, building small businesses even before they left high school. Now they would see their employers as places to collect skills and build resumes. Ultimately, they are more loyal to their professions than their employers. Third, they would live a more balanced and personally fulfilling life. Having seen their parents burn out working long hours, weekends, and holidays (often foregoing family time and sacrificing their health), they became committed to having more fun along the way, leaving work behind at the office, and devoting more time to family and friends.

> *"We have to adapt to the needs of a new generation. For example, they still need to be challenged, but we are having difficulty getting people to move locations! Younger folks still have drive to get ahead, but a greater appreciation for work-life balance."*
> –Ron Thiry, Vice President of Operations

Older generations have been both frustrated by this turn of events and jealous of the new workforce's freedom. Retiring Baby Boomers are adopting many of these practices themselves, particularly trying to find better work-life balance in their "golden years."

As a result, the contemporary manager is dealing with a new kind of workforce. Your labor force is technologically smarter compared to older generations, focused on their own pursuits as much as (or more than) the goals of your organization, ready and willing to leave their jobs at the "drop of a hat," and committed to having a balanced life.

They are unwilling to work the long, erratic and sometimes unnecessary schedules prescribed by their bosses. If you try to exert too much "command and control," micromanage their work, or pay too little attention to their needs, they will either withhold effort or simply pick up or leave.

> *"I assumed that my new staff had the same work ethic I did, the same priorities as mine, but that was a big mistake. I was dealing with a very different generation than my own with different values. It was a hard lesson."*
>
> –Kathy Stover, Assistant Vice President
> of Clinical R&D

To be successful in this brave new workplace, new managers should view today's employees more like volunteers than paid employees. After all, they don't have to work for you, they aren't planning to stay for long, and they have taken back control of how they spend their work and family time.

Managers of actual volunteers know this reality already and have learned to adapt their approach accordingly. If they don't treat their precious volunteers carefully, they simply fail to materialize the next day.

If this were to happen, they would be constantly searching for replacements, spending entirely too much time recruiting and training, and too little time achieving the goals of the organization. When these things occur, work simply doesn't get done and the mission is summarily not accomplished.

Just because your staff earns a paycheck, don't think for a minute that you're not a manager of "volunteers." You are.

As a result, you have to be even more adept at leading people than managers of the past. Some of the same principles apply, but your success as leader is more dependent on your informal authority and team leadership than it ever was before.

> *"As a young manager, you think the world is revolving around you, but it's revolving around your people."*
>
> –Tom Mettlach, Operations Manager

Really Get to Know Them

The workforce is more than ever a collection of individuals with varied needs, goals and aspirations. In many ways, these people are your primary customers, the ones you work through to serve your ultimate ones. With your external customers, you certainly want to build relationships, help solve problems, and fill their orders! But with employees, the relationship is even more complex and significant.

Your lives are connected now by common goals and needs. You depend upon each other to achieve needed results. When there are hard feelings, morale problems, and team issues, your volunteers leave. They might not leave physically, but their discretionary effort falls to nil.

Also, your time is shared in close proximity to one another, and what each of you does causes ripple effects on the others, some good and some bad. You're forced to cope with each other's foibles for a large percentage of your day. Customer relationships are transactional and actually more superficial. Team relationships are much more immediate and interdependent.

Since your success depends others, the first order of business is to get to know your people as individuals and to foster professional relationships. While this may seem obvious, new managers get pulled in a lot of directions, and it's easy to get distracted from this very fundamental requirement.

I am not recommending that you ask directly personal questions about subordinates' health, family history, or their deepest darkest secrets. That would clearly be too personal, and if they start to volunteer that kind of information, it would behoove you to gently point out that while you appreciate their trust, you would rather not be privy to facts that would be inappropriate for you to know. You're not their best friend but their manager, someone who cares about them as people but is not intimately involved in their personal lives.

In addition to what's already on their resume, the following would be generally acceptable and helpful things to learn about your subordinates:

- Why they work where they do
- Publicly visible things you have in common
- Immediate family names
- Pets and hobbies
- Career goals, personal goals, and aspirations
- Learning styles and preferences
- Things they are proud of
- Things that they enjoy about work
- Things they dislike about work
- Things they are concerned about that are related to work
- What motivates or demotivates them

- Perceived developmental needs related to work
- Their expectations of you

"Work your tail off to get to know them, each and every person and not just their birthdays. Get to know about them, what's important to them, what their goals are. People don't care how much you know until they know how much you care."

–Jeff Samford, President

Understanding Motivations

I recently volunteered to help the Boy Scouts of America. This wasn't the first time. I had already been a volunteer in my troop and district but felt compelled to do something more on the council level. But I wasn't sure what it might be. So I made an appointment to see the Scout Executive for the Council and explored the possibility with him. After checking my background, he immediately demonstrated a key competency for savvy contemporary leaders. He started to explore my interests.

Tell me about your work. What are you interested in doing? What would be beneficial to you? What do you think of these options? Which of these is most appealing and why? What would be the most fun? How could these options support your goals while also serving Scouting?

His approach may seem logical and obvious in this context, but it should be equally apropos in the workplace and not just at the point of hiring. You see, the executive knew something that we all need to recognize when managing others. He knew that if he found the right fit for me, I would be more likely to stay and add real value to the business.

"It is a failure to understand that the real way to drive performance is to be highly dedicated to the people aspects of the job. The new manager tends to think it is all about the deliverables. The focus is on reports and phone calls. If you're not careful, the people aspects of the job fall way down the list."

–Jim Horton, Sales Manager

As Ron Thiry put it, "We tend to assume that other people are motivated the way we are. It takes a while to appreciate that others may not have the same needs that trip your trigger." As a result, you need to work hard to discover what your people are truly interested in, what really excites them about their work, and what causes them to have a terrific day on the job. You can ask them forthrightly (i.e., what are your motivations?). However, you might not get an accurate response.

People don't always know exactly what kind of work is inspiring to them. They may just want a paycheck and some benefits in a field where they have some qualifications. They might not be in a particularly stimulating role right now, or they may be working in an organization that is not the best overall fit for their values. If this is the case, it will be hard to make their work compelling. Also, your team members might not have a clear idea of their goals or interests, or they might just tell you what they think you want to hear. In any case, you'll have to work harder to discover their intrinsic motivations if you want to see their best work.

"If I force people to play music, I might get 'Chopsticks.' But if they are inspired and believe their

*work has value and makes a contribution, I am likely
to get 'Piano Concerto No. 1.'"*
                    –Anthony Romanello, County Administrator

There are some psychometric tests that help illuminate what these might be, but you can get a good idea by asking the right questions and listening very carefully. Instead of asking directly about their motivations, ask them to tell you stories that will give you clues about what those motivators might be. By eliciting stories about jobs or tasks that were fun, interesting and significant to them, you can then listen for the patterns in their responses. These are the clues to a person's true motivations. Here are some sample questions.

What were some jobs that were meaningful to you? Tell me about some projects that were particularly fun or inspiring. What was a time period or specific day when you couldn't wait to get out of bed and get to work on something? Where have you made the biggest difference for something or somebody? What was the best job, or project, you ever had and why?

You'll have to work harder to find out their intrinsic motivations if you want to see their best work.

The themes will start to emerge in their stories. Some will tell stories about how they helped people solve problems and got satisfaction from that. Others will explain how they enjoyed new and big challenges that no else had grappled with before. Still others might talk about the importance of

getting and keeping things organized. The list of possibilities may be endless, but Dr. Robert Hogan identifies the top 10 motivational drivers in his assessment of motives, values, preferences, and interests. They are aesthetics, affiliation, altruism, commerce, fun, power, recognition, science, security, and tradition.

> *"If I had understood sooner that people are motivated by different things, I would have saved a lot of bruises. Maybe someone told me that early on, but it didn't sink in until later."*
> –Ron Thiry, Vice President of Operations

No matter what pattern you find in people's stories, the goal is to uncover your subordinates' individual motivations so that you can tap into these more fully. As a manager, you can shape the individual jobs in your purview by assigning work that fits staff interests. Even small adjustments can produce big returns. When you do that, you simultaneously improve your staff's work lives and generate greater productivity.

You can also tap into their discretionary effort by discovering their job ambitions. Where do you see yourself in this organization in the next few years? What would be the perfect job for you? At this point, what's the next rung on your particular career ladder? Is there a role around here that interests you in the short or long term? When you look at open positions, which ones are the most attractive to you? Is there something that you want to learn that we can accommodate in some way?

Knowing where your staff wants to go in the organization or in their career, you can link their aspirations to many aspects of their work. You can give them delegations that will help them grow their skills and get the visibility they need. You can put them in touch with mentors in those fields and assign developmental resources that will help them prepare for such roles, whether they are in your organization or another one.

> *"The most successful managers focus on their relationships first. Let your ego fall and build relationships. This is the meat and potatoes of good leadership. You have to know enough about them so you can–in fact–set them up for success. It's about genuine caring for knowing what's important to your people."*
>
> –Jeff Samford, President

In any case, you will be motivating a valuable resource now and capturing more of their discretionary effort in their current role.

Put Your People First

Good leaders don't expect loyalty, they earn it. "Your first thought should be about your people's needs versus your own. It's a mindset shift from when you worked as an individual," said Denise Kasper. This is even true in organizations where formal authority is engendered in the most absolute terms.

Col. Don Sowder explained, "A good commander realizes that the only way to accomplish the mission is with the men. The second lieutenant is the boss; he can do almost anything he wants, get at the head of the chow line, pick the best

quarters, etc. But good commanders should eat last, give up creature comforts so his men can have them. That earns people's respect. That's the difference between directing and leading."

"As you become a manager, it is not about you anymore. You show up for your team. You lead them in ways to make them most productive. To do this, you have to give up some things for yourself."

–Sarah Gravitt-Baese, Vice President

Donna Blatecky gave this advice to pass along, "Give people credit! Do not let your bosses think you did it if the credit should go to your staff. The only way I look good is when my staff makes me look good. Really take care of your staff. Make sure your staff are appreciated and recognized appropriately. You don't need to have the light shine on you directly. Let the light shine on your staff for their contributions and successes; it will reflect back on you."

On a daily basis, you can put your people first by giving them the following:

- Credit, even if it might have flowed to you otherwise
- Visibility, even if it might have been yours to take
- Time, even if you don't have it
- Resources, even if you could have used them yourself
- Opportunities, even if they mean you lose a good person
- Chances to learn, even though there is risk to you
- Feedback, even though it might be hard to deliver

"Surround yourself with good people and learn to confer with them. Consider your job as letting them shine."

–Judith B. Douglas, Client Industry Executive

Being Seen as a Leader Requires being Seen

Legendary basketball coach John Wooden once said, "Don't mistake activity for achievement." Your days will be filled with activity, almost all of which you will be able to rationalize as important, even critical at that very moment. The urgency of these activities, some of them very high priority tasks, can easily consume your day and put your people on the "back burner." You have to guard against this temptation, or you will find yourself as a leader without followers.

"I started to get out of touch with people," said Mike Bogenschutz. "I didn't recognize the importance of being visible, just being present. I had to make that a priority. Just get out and talk to people. After getting back in that groove again, people started to say, 'nice to see you out here again.'"

I once had a coaching client who was an executive in a hospital, and he was so focused on his tasks that his relationships almost cost him his job. I was told by human resources that he was universally despised by his subordinates, had a reputation for being aloof, and was a poor communicator. He was in real trouble unless he could "get his act together" and fast.

When I met the individual, I started to wonder if this was the right person. He was conversant, funny, and open to my

questions. We shared our work histories, information about our families and hobbies for much longer than usual, the sign of easily-built rapport. He was easy to talk with and interested in how I could help. He was also taken aback when I fully explained the reputation I was told about and the reason I was there. He seemed genuinely surprised, even shocked, but was not defensive about my offer of assistance.

After a number of interviews with his staff, there were very few new issues to report but lots of implications to talk with him about. It was true that his employees disliked him immensely, but not because of what they knew about him; it was what they didn't know that was such a problem. His employees resented the fact that he never seemed interested in them, rushed past their cubicles on the way to his office, entered and exited the building through a side entrance, and worked with his door closed all day.

When I reported the data, he agreed that these were his behaviors, but he didn't realize what an impact they were having. However, because he cared about being a better manager, he was open to some coaching, able to adapt his style, and became much more visible and accessible to his staff. As his employees got to know him better, the impact of his detached behavior eventually wore off and relations improved. But it took some time and real effort on his part to make that happen. To be seen as a leader, he had to be visible as a person.

My client was very focused on his work and actually trusted his employees to do their jobs. His philosophy was that if they needed him, they'd certainly let him know it. Otherwise, he didn't want to interrupt their work or "breathe down their neck." He made the faulty assumption that if he didn't need much contact with them, then they didn't need much contact with him.

To be seen as a leader, he had to be visible as a person.

His staff wasn't asking to be micromanaged. They just wanted to connect with their boss, to be assured that he was in touch with their needs and concerns, and to know that they were important to him and the organization. If you're muttering about how "touchy feely" that sounds, then read on. This whole chapter is for you.

> *"The soft side of employee relations is so important. You have to be truly concerned about your employees and pay attention to the details. It's very time consuming but absolutely necessary."*
> –Tom Mettlach, Operations Manager

Having an "open-door policy" is a start, but it is too passive an approach to be successful by itself. It's like assuming "silence is consent" in a group decision-making process, when it can mean just the opposite!

You need to be proactive at being in touch with your people. Plan your day to include routine contacts with your subordinates. "Make the rounds" even when you don't have

a formal agenda of good or bad news. Ask questions and listen carefully to the answers. Get to know people as they get to know you. Your contacts don't have to be long, but they have to be frequent. You should "take the pulse" of your team and know their vital signs, so that when something is amiss, you know it right away.

As you set up meetings with your staff and discuss their performance, Conni Morse cautioned, "Be careful not to spend too much time with 'problem employees.' All other employees will see you doing that and will wonder why they get so much attention and help. High performers are not likely to ask for help, but they need it too and will put it to better use."

> *"Step back and build relationships across departments early on rather than waiting for the opportunities to dictate themselves. When I took this job at law, I didn't make a concerted effort to go sit down with others to learn. It's better to improve those relationships right up front rather than over time. You won't be seen as a leader if people don't see enough of you."*
>
> –Bill Galanko, Vice President - Law

Demonstrate that You Care

I was a public affairs officer for a paper mill at one time in my career. It was terrific preparation for leadership, but without formal training for the role, I was completely on my own to figure out what to do and how best to do it. I found out much later that this is how most leadership lessons are

learned—the hard way. It was during this time that I discovered how important "the little things" are to people.

When I heard this story from Larry Julian, a Leadership Coach and Consultant, I knew I would use it to help make a point. "In the mid-1970s, I had the opportunity to fulfill a childhood dream of driving an 18-wheeler cross country. We would make a trip each week from North Carolina to the West coast and back, and every time we returned to home base, the owner would hand us our paychecks, shake our hands, and thank us for the great job that we were doing. It was a simple gesture, yet it was powerful in its impact, and inspired a rare level of loyalty among his employees.

"Later, I started a new career in corporate America, starting on the ground floor as production supervisor in a manufacturing environment. The normal practice was to hand each employee their paycheck at the end of the week. During my training period, I noticed that most of the current supervisors simply delivered the checks with no positive comments, in fact, some would often make a joke about it, such as suggesting that the individual had not really earned it. I determined that I would set a different standard and use the lessons learned from some self-identified 'good old boys,' from Mount Airy, NC. I would hand each person their check, shake their hand, and thank them for their hard work that week. Needless to say, I received some strange looks and responses the first few times I did it. Yet, years later, I learned that my name still comes up in that facility for this simple act of appreciation."

"The three fundamental questions individuals continually ask about their new managers are: Do I trust you? Do you care about me, and are you committed?"

–Ken Robertson, Human Resources Director

As a leadership consultant, I've had numerous occasions to interview people about effective leadership they have witnessed. Whether it was hospitals, government agencies, or high-tech outfits, the themes have always been the same. Even in the most hardcore workplaces, like certain manufacturing environments and the United States military, participants have consistently revealed that one of the most compelling attributes of the best leaders they have known is that "they care about their people."

This may be one of the most important aspects of leadership, yet it is one of the least talked about. It's too "touchy feely" to be palatable in many places, but when you ask and listen, it's what people talk about. While it's consistently valued in leaders, it's also the one of the most difficult—if not impossible—to "train." It's more of a trait that great leaders have and others lack.

While you can attend sensitivity and interpersonal skills training, it's difficult to codify and train the behaviors that emulate "caring." It's more of a value system that is deeply held, and cannot be successfully faked for long. The presence of caring or the lack thereof becomes obvious to others over time. Hardship and emergencies seem to illuminate its presence very fast. Maybe that's why people in dangerous occupations know so much about it.

"If someone had a health problem, he would visit any employee at home or in the hospital, just to stop in and ask if they needed anything. I applied that lesson later in my career. Anytime someone was hurt, I required that a manager go with them in the ambulance until a family member could take over. People are not just numbers."

–Jim Horton, Sales Manager

While it was not "dangerous," I did experience a personal emergency that drove this lesson home. I was once part of building a new paper mill, a "greenfield start up." It was going to be the biggest of its kind the world, and I was involved in the workforce design, hiring, and training. In the midst of a very hectic Friday afternoon, I got a call in the field from my boss, who was working in another state.

He had gotten word of an all-hands meeting at the home office. Not unusual in and of itself, but he had also heard that the state governor was going to meet with our company president at about the same time. It turned out that our operation was being sold, the project was being canceled, and our jobs were being eliminated in the next few hours.

The small community where we would have worked had their hopes for hundreds of new jobs dashed in one phone call. I had my hands full that weekend with public relations from the fallout. But the part of the story I want to highlight is about how my boss spent the next few days.

In what might have been his last few hours on the job, he was on the phone to other plant managers, subsidiaries all over the country, getting people out of bed and rattling cages

to uncover jobs and to place his people in them before too many hours passed and those opportunities were lost. At a time when he could easily have been angry, depressed and self-involved, he was looking out for his staff so that we would not have to suffer uncertainty or displacement for long. It was the kind of action that is taken only by someone who cares for his people.

Obviously, this left an indelible impression on me and taught me something important about what it takes to be a truly effective leader. Later, I would hear this same theme echoed by lab technicians, heavy equipment operators, and U.S. Army Rangers. If you care, show it. If you don't, get a different job.

Rowing in the Same Direction

Outside of a common enemy or an emergency, one thing gets people moving in the same direction faster than anything else, that's a shared vision. Leaders must envision and communicate how things will be in the future; knowing what success looks like gives everyone the same target to shoot for. This can be done a number of ways, but it has to get done.

When people have a shared vision, they start pulling in the same direction, even without the leader being there or telling anyone what to do. "Have a vision for how you want your group to be operating six months from now," said Denise G. Kasper. "It is critical for a leader to be able to clearly articulate this for the team. By painting a picture, it helps them make choices about what to do, how to prioritize."

When organizational surveys are taken, "communications" tops the list nearly every time. It's always there because it's important to people and it's hard to do well. If you want to keep your team moving in the same direction, you need to over communicate with them, and that means listening as much as explaining. Repeat your key points eight times through different media. Ask questions and have them reiterate what you said in writing.

"Take time to provide positive feedback," said Tom Mettlach. "Good managers know it's hard and time consuming to do, but they do it anyway. The business isn't evaluating you for writing a nice note, but that's the kind of thing that drives the business."

Even as we find new and faster ways to connect electronically, there will still be one form of communication that's timeless -- personal communication. It has yet to be duplicated. Make the phone call or go see someone face to face on occasion, not just when delivering bad news but to say thank you. Spend time with the people you care about. It's the only way to prove your sincerity.

Bret Anderson, a Regional Sales Director, said, "What separates good from great managers is the discretionary effort given by their teams. If they don't think their manager is on their side, working for them, then they are not going to give that extra effort." Your results depend upon how much of this valuable resource they are willing to give you, and their decision will be based upon how well you lead and manage your relationships, not how much of a hero you can be to your boss.

MISTAKE #2
ASSIGNMENTS FOR A SUCCESSFUL ASCENT TO MANAGEMENT

❑ Read *Love 'em or Lose 'em: Getting Good People to Stay* by Beverly L. Kaye. Extract at least 10 key principles you plan to apply on the job.

❑ Get to know each person on your team personally, their work history, strengths, and weaknesses.

❑ Regularly ask what interests them, what makes them excited about their work, and what their most proud accomplishments are. Their answers provide the clues you need to determine what's in it for them.

❑ Enrich their jobs in the short term by including work that is motivational for them. Help them align their interests over the long-term so they have the best job fit and greatest likelihood of success.

❑ Build a shared vision, starting with your own as a "straw man," getting feedback from your team, and adapting it to become a shared description of how things will be when you are successful as a group.

❑ Break this down into a checklist that can be rated annually to measure progress. Team members can rank each element on a scale of 1-10 and give examples of what's going well and what could go better.

❑ Give credit to your team when things go well, and take the blame when things don't go so well.

❑ Use personal communications whenever possible, especially when there's good or bad news to share.

❑ Involve people when making changes that affect them or developing plans that they will have to execute.

"Just because you can do it
— and want to—
doesn't mean you should."

–Tom Davidson

The Fool-it-Yourselfer
Failing to delegate and develop others

My wife and I live in a 40-year-old house, and while it's not a "fixer-upper," it does have some of the usual repair and maintenance problems that need occasional attention. Some of these are relatively high-cost projects that we plan to get to over time, while others have more immediate consequences. I'm lucky she is good with tools because there is always something for her to work on!

For instance, we currently have some peeling paint on the ceiling in our living room. While that might not sound like a big deal, the ceiling is 17-feet in the air, which puts it well out of reach of standard ladders and extension poles. We'll soon have to decide whether to tackle this one ourselves or find a contractor. As you would imagine, we have some questions to answer first:

- *Does this just require a patch, or is there a bigger problem causing the paint to "pop" like this?*
- *What is the actual size of the project, just the patch area, the entire ceiling, or the whole room?*
- *Is this something we're capable of doing ourselves, or does it take some special skills or equipment we would have to acquire?*
- *Do we even want to do this project, especially considering the ceiling height and safety concerns?*
- *What would it cost to have someone else do the repair?*
- *Can we afford it at this time, or will we have to live with it a while longer until we have the money and/or the time?*
- *What else would we do with that money if it were not spent on the ceiling repair?*
- *Will we learn something from doing this ourselves that will help us save money or time down the road?*
- *How significantly would it add to our enjoyment of the house?*
- *How long would it take, and would it tie up the room in significant ways, causing more problems?*

Why am I writing about my ceiling paint in a chapter on delegation?

I'm using this as an analogy because I think you may ask similar questions of yourself when deciding whether or not to do a home repair but *fail* to do so when faced with similar challenges at work. Also, I've found that new managers labor under certain false assumptions and *fool* themselves into believing that they should do work that really belongs in the hands of someone else. That's why Mistake #3 is called

"The Fool-it-Yourselfer," not simply "The Do-it-Yourselfer."

> *"All of a sudden you have all these new responsibilities, and you are not inclined to trust others or you don't have the confidence that others can do it as well as you. At the same time, you're anxious to demonstrate your skill and competence in the job. It's easy to go ahead and do it yourself, but that's not the job you were promoted to do."*
>
> –Mike Bogenschutz, VP Plant Operations

New managers fail to delegate sufficiently, because they feel it's risky. But the real risk comes from not delegating well or often. Here's what new managers report as their reasons for not delegating. Feel free to check your favorites:

New managers labor under certain false assumptions and fool themselves into believing that they should do work that really belongs in the hands of someone else.

❑ **Responsibility** – *Since I was promoted to oversee this work and because I was the best individual performer, it is my responsibility to get it done, even if that means doing it myself.*

❑ **Efficiency** - *Since I've done this many times before, I can do it faster than anyone else, so it would be most efficient for me to go ahead and do it myself.*

- ❑ **Effectiveness** - *Since everyone is very busy doing other things and delegating this to them would be a distraction, it would just be a lot easier to do it myself.*
- ❑ **Cost** – *Since I would have to show them what to do, look over their shoulder while they're doing it, and check the final product before it goes out the door anyway, it would be cheaper for everyone if I do it myself.*
- ❑ **Relationships** – *Since I'm new and still building positive relationships with my team, I don't want to appear too "bossy" or as if I don't want to pull my own weight, so I'll show them what a team player I am and do it myself.*
- ❑ **Quality** - *Since no one else can do this as well as I and the result will be a direct reflection on my performance, to make sure it's done right I better do it myself.*
- ❑ **Job Security** – *Since I just got promoted, I really need to look good and prove myself so that no one changes their mind, so to make sure they see that I'm on top of things, I better do it myself.*

Let's face it, high-performing individuals are used to doing things themselves, and many of them like it that way. They just don't know how much, until they become a manager and start to get separated from the hands-on work they enjoyed. New managers often find it difficult to go from "doer" to "manager of doers." It's not that the *skills* of delegation are that

> *It's not that the skills of delegation are that difficult to learn; it's that people don't initially see the reason or have the will to use them.*

difficult to learn. We will review those shortly. It's that people don't initially see the reason or that they lack sufficient *will* to use the skills to do it.

With that said, you might think I'm saying that you should never step in. That's not true, but the tendency of the new manager is to do far more of the hands-on work than they should. When you decide to step in, not delegate and do someone else's job for them, it should be for one of two reasons only, (1) to train them how to do it themselves and (2) to get through a real emergency. If you do it at other times, you're fooling yourself and undermining the effectiveness of the organization.

> *"I know I can do it quicker if I do it myself, but I also know that this is short-term thinking. I wish someone had told me earlier in my career to be patient and to look at the long term sooner. Just yesterday I had a receptionist doing some clerical work and she had to pin me down to show her some things about the e-files so she could do an important job. It took an hour I didn't think I had, but now she is really going to be able to do a lot more on her own."*
>
> –Doug Morgan, Human Resource Director

What's at stake

There's certainly a degree of truth in your reasons for holding on to the work; but when weighed against the organizational risks of not delegating, the benefits tend to pale by comparison. By doing too much yourself, you may temporarily avoid some inconveniences (real or imagined);

but you'll certainly multiply the following bigger-picture risks that new managers overlook and undervalue.

"For me it manifests as micromanaging, being too explicit about the how versus the what. It should always be a balance between directional and directive. That's the biggest change."

–Sarah Gravitt-Baese, Vice President

Responsibility

Your duty is to do your job so other people can do theirs. Of course that means that you do what is necessary to get things done, but this line of thinking usually leads to working harder not smarter. The bottom line is that if you're doing someone else's job (i.e., something that can and should be delegated), then the organization is paying you too much money and would be justified in demoting you back to your old position.

As discussed in Mistake #1, if you really want to do your duty, you'll learn that your new job involves developing people, getting resources, solving strategic problems, and mobilizing and motivating your team. If you're doing these things to any significant degree, you'll simply not have time to do someone else's job too, let alone those of ten other people.

Not only that, because you are taking yourself out of your real role, your bosses are forced to drop down a level to fill your shoes. They will have to stop what they're doing to do the reports you aren't getting done because you're on the

shop floor turning wrenches. Similarly, your boss' boss is then pulled down a notch and so forth.

> *"Even though it was easier for me to do the work just to get it done, I had to learn to step back and make sure the work was humming everywhere, that people had the training. I had to stop calculating the cases myself, which was hard because I'd just been there, and they felt like I'd left them floating without oars and was just sitting behind my desk with my feet up because they didn't see me doing their work. I had other work to do. The sooner you wrap your head around that, the more likely you will be to delegate effectively."*
>
> –Donna Blatecky, Deputy Director

By not delegating effectively, you're causing a ripple effect that undermines the effectiveness of the entire organization. A string of managers are forced to focus on less-than strategic problems, and the organization is weakened against the competition and less likely to achieve its goals.

If you're doing someone else's job, then

- No one is pursuing the necessary short- or long-term resources the team will need to do its job
- No one is coordinating the efforts of the team as a whole such that work falls between the cracks, is unnecessarily duplicated, or is executed inefficiently in any number of ways
- No one is building intricate relationships with other departments, vendors, and other stakeholders who can and will undermine your success

- No one is making contingency plans to mitigate risk, minimize downtime, or avoid the unnecessary loss of jobs down the road

If you're causing these things to happen, then not only should you be demoted, you should be fired! The organization is paying for a manager but getting a specialist that they could have gotten much cheaper. You're ripping off your own employer if you are spending time doing someone else's job. That's how serious this is. So if you want to do your duty, then learn to delegate appropriately.

"I should have trusted my staff more with responsibilities, but I frequently neglected to share them. I always felt that if the superintendent gave me a charge, I was responsible for its accomplishment. I would hold on to it to make sure it was done correctly. I should have delegated more to my staff to help them grow. They were certainly capable of assuming more responsibility than I shared."
–Hattie D. Webb, Ed.D., School Division
Central Office Leadership Team

Efficiency

From your vantage point as an individual contributor, it may seem faster to do it yourself, but this is a "slippery slope." You have to elevate your attention from your old perspective to that of your team as a whole. From the team perspective, you will lose efficiency over time if you don't delegate.

How do you measure the collective efficiency of your work unit? Outside of meeting specific goals, you and your team

are successful when your team can perform its work *without you*. But that doesn't mean they don't need you. They just need you for other things.

If you keep doing (and re-doing) their work, they learn to wait, work on something less productive, or drag things out until you do your usual trick of swooping in to save the day. Why should they even bother if they know you're going to snatch it out of their hands or rework what they've already done? Who could blame them?

If you still feel you have to do it yourself because others are less capable or practiced at doing a quality job, then the solution is not to perpetuate the problem by doing it yourself but rather to get them the tools and/or training they need to elevate their skills and results. How are they going to learn if you keep doing it for them? They won't!

> *"New managers make two mistakes here. One is taking on too much too early because they tend to be overachievers and want it piled on. The other is not knowing how or not being willing to delegate. Therefore, even though he has a team, he is working 15 hours a day and his team members are going home on time!"*
>
> –Kurt Frank, Vice President IT Portfolio Office

Effectiveness

You might think it's easier to do it yourself, less distracting to the team. Yes, delegation is hard and has some risks, but it will be a lot harder on you when you burn out, overburden

your personal and family life, and get mired in other people's work without doing your own.

It will also be much harder on your team because they will feel stuck in their jobs, mistrusted, and stagnating rather than developing for the future. *The more of the work you take from your subordinates, the more your people will let you.* Unwittingly, new managers dig the hole deeper and deeper. As this burden grows, the farther you stray from your real job, the management position you were hired to do. Ironically, the failure you were trying to avoid becomes the result anyway.

> *The more of the work you take from your subordinates, the more your people will let you.*

As for the long term, if you're constantly distracted from your real job, you will learn your new role more slowly than you will otherwise. You remain a beginner much longer, hurting your results over time, and leaving the door wide open for someone else to get promoted ahead of you.

Costs

Yes, doing it yourself can be faster than delegating the work to someone else, at least in the short run. It's also faster for you to do your children's homework, more expedient to duct tape a leaking hose, and quicker to ignore a chronic pain in your neck. But what are the consequences?

Let's say your daughter needs an "A" on a term paper to pass an important course. As a truly concerned parent, you might help with the research, develop an outline, contribute to the actual writing, and edit the final product. As a result, you might help get the needed "A," but at what cost?

Now your daughter will continue whatever poor study habits, lack of focus, or laziness that got her into this mess in the first place. As a result, this crisis will happen again and again in one form or another. She will probably remain dependent upon you for her work and blame you for her failures. You have also modeled poor work ethics and other bad behaviors, like cheating, shirking responsibility, and not being accountable for your actions.

If no one is ready to take over your position, then you are less likely to get promoted anytime soon yourself!

The consequences of poor delegation at work are easier to overlook than the ones in the example above. One hidden cost has already been mentioned, the one associated with pulling down a string of managers from their real jobs because you aren't doing yours.

Another hidden cost is the lack of learning that takes place when you barge in and do the work for someone else. Part of your real job is to develop the talent in your area of responsibility, and the best way people learn is from on-the-

job experience. If you are not providing these experiences to your staff, then you're robbing them of needed opportunities to learn, and you're diminishing the pool of talent available to your organization for future positions. If that doesn't concern you, maybe this will. If no one is ready to take over your position, then you are less likely to get promoted anytime soon yourself!

> *"I didn't delegate nearly enough, but I learned over time to ask myself, 'Is this something someone else can be doing?' I needed to be doing what no one else could do; that was my responsibility. Simply put, you must delegate what someone else can and should be doing."*
> –Denise G. Kasper, Human Resources Director

Other hidden costs are known as "opportunity costs," a term from economics that has broad application in business. In economics, opportunity cost is the dollar value of the "next best" alternative that is bypassed for the chosen course of action. It is a universal problem that arises from the need to make tradeoffs because time and resources are always scarce. When applied to the concept of delegation, it's the value of what you *might have been* doing if you were not tied up doing what you *chose* to be doing.

If you choose to take personal responsibility for some aspect of the workflow for yourself, then your opportunity cost is the next best use of your time. For instance, you might choose to troubleshoot a maintenance problem (something you are known to be good at but others are also capable of doing), but you *might have* chosen to use that time finding a

better service provider for your team who would have improved quality, timeliness, or reliability. While you were busy troubleshooting, you lost the opportunity to find significant help and savings from a new vendor.

> *"Young managers don't understand the metric that if they train someone to replace themselves, that's a good thing. You can't get promoted if you don't have someone to fill your spot."*
>
> –Chris Burgess, President & CEO

The hidden costs of poor delegation practices are harder to measure, but that doesn't mean they don't exist and should not be taken into consideration.

Relationships

Delegating work to others can put a strain on your relationships but not the way you might think. Relationships might be stressed for a short time when you delegate hard work, but they are more likely to be damaged long term when you

- Dump tasks on individuals without adequate training, tools, guidance or support
- Overload staff without prioritizing or eliminating something extraneous
- Delegate to a few select people, ignoring others
- Keep the interesting, fun, and/or high-profile work for yourself
- Make it difficult for staff to learn new skills
- Limit their visibility in the organization
- Keep their resumes from growing

Adding insult to injury, you send an unintended but powerful message when you fail to delegate. You are essentially broadcasting that you don't trust your people. Your *in*actions speak louder than your words. If you don't trust them, they won't trust you, and your relationship will be deteriorating while you thought it was growing.

> *"New managers don't trust others as much as they need to. They try to control information and do everything themselves. As I have gotten older and grayer, I have started to trust everybody until they prove otherwise."*
>
> *–Chris Burgess, President & CEO*

These factors can quickly foster listless and restless work groups, especially if you have good people on your team who quite naturally want to advance and prosper more rapidly. If they aren't getting those opportunities, they will very likely find a way off your team and maybe out of your organization completely.

Quality

Be honest with yourself. Are you really the only one on your team who can produce a quality job? Because if that's the case, then you have bigger problems to solve than learning how to delegate. You have to learn how to hire, train, and motivate more effectively!

Nevertheless, when it comes to delegation, you have legitimate concerns regarding whether your supervisor will be satisfied with your results. After all, they write your performance reviews, and that affects your pay and

trajectory in the organization. I understand that, but your manager is unusually shortsighted if he or she expects you to handle personally too many aspects of your team's production. A good manager will be looking for *how* you achieved your results, not just *what* results you accomplished.

Your manager will be looking for evidence of the following:

- How you built your team and its teamwork
- How you developed your people
- How effectively the team operates without you
- How you spend your time—fighting fires or solving more strategic problems
- How fast you are learning your job and becoming ready for new challenges

The ultimate reputation you want is as someone who can get superior results with their team while contributing talented people to the rest of the organization. Lack of delegation will earn you the reputation of being a micromanager, a short-term thinker, and a lone ranger who is unable or unwilling to develop a team. If you continue to put expediency ahead of efficiency, effectiveness, and quality, then you're missing the big picture.

Job Security

It's true, you were hired to do a job. Someone took a chance on you, and you don't want to let them down. Also, you may be in the spotlight more than most for a period of time. After all, you're new and somewhat vulnerable to criticism as you get your feet wet and start flexing your leadership skills, perhaps for the first time. It's understandable for you

to feel as though you need to make a good first impression and are careful about having your "i's dotted and t's crossed," but this is yet another trap you may fall into.

If you're too worried about job security, you're likely to hold on too tightly to the tasks of your team, to exert too much control over the details, and to micromanage your able staff. True job security comes from successful team efforts, not the heroic deeds and sleepless nights of the leader.

Show that you can mobilize a team to achieve breakthrough results, and you will have all the job security that's possible in this day and age. Hold on too tightly, and you might just become expendable.

Now that you know the consequences of not delegating, this section is to help you do it well. As with many other parts of your new management job, delegation is both art and science. There are some very specific principles that need to be present for a delegation to be successful. These will be reviewed next.

> *True job security comes from successful team efforts, not the heroic deeds and sleepless nights of the leader.*

In addition to the basics, the truly artful manager is creative in the assignments he crafts, generates them in partnership with his subordinates, inserts learning objectives into his delegations, and gets multiple benefits from each task. When you're using

delegations to full advantage, you'll be making the most of your team's talents, both in the short and long run.

Assessment

Effective delegation begins with an accurate assessment of your staff's current and needed skills, and that begins with an understanding of where your work group is today and where it needs to be in the future. For example, at one point in my career, I worked with a group of human resource professionals who had been groomed and slotted in various positions based on their functional expertise. Human resources is a large field with many sub-professions, and this strategy fit the organization's small size and steady growth plans.

But the organization was growing and shifting priorities at a rapid rate, so the strategy of the human resources team became one that needed "generalists" more than "specialists." People were going to need to solve problems outside of their usual expertise and functional areas of responsibility. They needed to become "internal consultants" on a wider array of challenges.

They weren't necessarily opposed to this, but it meant that they had to start doing new things and stop doing others. As a result, the delegations needed to be changed. Instead of always picking the traditional "expert," I started asking non-experts to take the lead on certain projects, using the traditional experts as advisors. Did this take longer? Yes. Did this risk quality output at least in the short term? Yes. Was this risky because my performance was being judged in

the short term? Yes. But it was also a necessary adjustment to a "big picture" change in the nature of our business.

In addition to a broad understanding of the situation, you also need to assess each individual, not just once but continuously. The following three-way test is easy to remember: ready, willing and able. Your answer has to be at least partially affirmative in all three areas for you to have the best chance at a successful delegation.

> *"One of my proudest moments was when I was stationed in the Pentagon. I went on leave to Washington State for three weeks and convinced the Colonel I worked for to allow Captain Mary Conners, who reported to me, to be in charge in my absence. The Colonel didn't even know who she was at the time, but when I got back, I asked how she did. He said, 'She did great, better at some things than you were!' I happily said, 'I told you so!' When I was reassigned from the Pentagon to attend the Army's Command General College, Colonel McCarthy selected Captain Conners as my replacement, simply because she had the opportunity to demonstrate her talent while I was on leave for a few weeks. The lessons for me were, it's okay to take extended leave; it's a great developmental opportunity for others; and it's great to see others shine when given the opportunity to do so."*
> –Ken Robertson, Human Resources Director

Ready

Is your delegate ready for the assignment? If you are a perfectionist, you may *never* feel your staff is "ready," but there's little need for perfectionists in management positions. Even your veteran team members have yet to do everything, and these days, there's always something new. As a result, it's unlikely your subordinates will ever be fully ready for their assignments, and the same is true for you when you're on the receiving end of a delegation.

Nevertheless, the target of your delegation has to be at least minimally prepared for the assignment. Otherwise you may be setting them up for failure. By minimally ready, I mean they need to have sufficient knowledge, skills and abilities to do the task. If they don't, then you need to lay some groundwork before delegating the work.

If you don't have a clear sense of their readiness, here are some questions you might ask yourself:

- ❏ Have they had basic training, mentoring or coaching on this subject?
- ❏ Have they ever done this assignment before in your organization?
- ❏ Have they ever done this task before in a different job or organization?
- ❏ Have they ever done anything like this before?
- ❏ Have they ever done a piece of the pending assignment before?
- ❏ Have they seen others do it or had other close proximity to this work in the past?
- ❏ What was the result of their involvement, if any?

If there's little evidence of readiness, you might step back and give this assignment to someone else, but consider including this person in part of the assignment now so they'll be more ready the next time you need them. If the person you had in mind for the task is not ready because of knowledge or skills, you might also consider providing that person with education or training on this subject.

Moreover, if you're having trouble finding someone on your team who is at least minimally prepared for the delegation, then you may have a significant gap in education and training on your entire team.

> *"The best indicator of my success is when people are ready to take over my job. This means I have managed to create my own successor. Accomplishments are great, but their readiness is the real indicator of how well you trained and developed your people."*
>
> –Conni Morse, Marketing Consultant

Willing

Is your delegate willing to take on the assignment? There's little point in delegating a task to someone who is unwilling, unmotivated, or resentful of executing it. Doing so will cause two problems. In *The Notebooks of Lazarus Long*, Author Robert Heinlein puts it this way, "Never try to teach a pig to sing; it wastes your time and it annoys the pig."

Be careful of your assumptions here. Staff may not be willing or motivated, even though you think they are. This can happen if they are intimidated in some way, or if they are so anxious to please that they say "yes" to everything

without question. It's also possible you may believe they're unwilling simply because they are less vocal than other subordinates.

> *"Don't be afraid to change the job versus change the job holder. Change the organization chart, the department structure, or the job responsibilities to keep a good person."*
>
> –Dave Winter, HR Consultant

As a card-carrying introvert, I found this out firsthand. Early in my management career, I was much less vocal than my counterparts. As a result, my interests were less well known to my superiors, and I was not "top of mind" when new or developmental assignments came along.

It wasn't until I had been passed over a few times that my frustration built up enough to protest noticeably, and I was given a chance to do something different. As it turned out, this opened the floodgates of opportunities and ultimately led to my changing career paths and ascending in leadership roles much more rapidly than otherwise would have been the case.

Here are some questions to ask yourself to test your delegates' willingness to perform:

- ❑ What is this person's level of risk aversion in general?
- ❑ How active has this individual been at attaining new knowledge or skills?
- ❑ Has this person proactively expressed interest in this type of work?

- ❑ What has been their response when you asked about their level of interest in this type of assignment?
- ❑ What are your potential delegate's personal interests, goals and motivations?
- ❑ Will this delegation contribute in some way to helping them reach one or more of these aspirations?
- ❑ What personal risks is this person taking if they accept this responsibility?
- ❑ Have they had a bad experience with this type of work in the past?
- ❑ What is their reputation for reliability?
- ❑ What evidence do you have that they can be resourceful?

If your potential delegate has been unreliable, uninspired, or unusually cautious about doing new things in the past, you're probably better off finding someone else to do the job. This may be especially true if the task is new, groundbreaking, high visibility, or otherwise risky. Such an individual may be better off in well-defined, stable, and niche-oriented roles that leverage their particular strengths.

> *"At district meetings for several years, I did the whole thing myself, not using the experience of the reps. I did all the planning and was totally exhausted running things. But I noticed other managers out in the hallways talking and doing business while I was running around doing all these details. I later realized that I didn't trust anyone else. The biggest lesson I learned from Tim was, "You are no longer a doer; you are a manager of doers."*
>
> –Jeffrey Bolea, District Sales Manager

Also be aware that "willingness" changes over time. Circumstances may have changed. As a result of some life event, pending changes in the organization, changing economic conditions, or the fact that they now have a more supportive boss, someone might wish to step forward more bravely and dependably than in the past. If you're unsure about willingness, you might make your first few delegations relatively minor in scope, then continue your assessment over time.

Able

Is your delegate able to execute the assignment? By this I mean are there barriers that need to be addressed, mitigated, or removed? Perhaps the most common example of this dilemma is when the subordinate is already overloaded with high-priority assignments. This tends to happen when you have very few people to delegate to or when the manager has favored one person with assignments more than others.

> *"Delegation is a needed skill up and down the organization. Some over-delegate, abdicating their responsibilities. Others try to do it all themselves. There is a skill that needs to be learned and a permission that needs to be granted by the culture of the organization."*
> –Carol Anderson, Chief Learning Officer

This can cause significant unfairness and strife among the team. Your "stars" can slough off their routine work to others, burdening them with what might be considered low-level or mundane tasks while the "favorites" continue to get the choice, interesting, fun or high-visibility assignments.

You might need to redistribute other delegations to make room for the new assignments, taking care to redeploy the fun, interesting, and high-visibility work more evenly to the rest of the team.

The days of slack time, extra staff, and multiple assistants are long past in most contemporary organizations, so coping with this capacity issue can be the most daunting element of the three-way test. Here are some questions to ask when assessing this component:

❑ Are your team's short-term and long-term goals clear, measurable, and in full alignment with the organization's goals and strategy?

❑ What is the true priority of the potential delegation, and how does it compare to other work in process?

❑ How is your staff really spending its time, and is it focused on high-priority goals?

❑ Is the work spread evenly and fairly across the work unit?

❑ Beyond capacity, what barriers could be in your delegate's way to success (i.e., systems, organizational politics, resistance, access to resources)?

❑ Have you done all you can to minimize or remove these barriers?

❑ Can the task be broken down into smaller components and shared among several delegates?

❑ Might some of the task be accomplished now and some later?

❑ Have you asked the potential delegate what else they would need from you to be successful?

The three-way assessment test might seem like a long process, but experienced managers learn to go through these checklists quickly, sometimes postponing delegations or changing their mind in mid-course. You'll begin to see the big picture of each delegation more clearly over time. You'll also be able to prevent readiness problems, understand willingness challenges, and head-off barriers that prevent successful execution.

Develop

As the manager, you'll often find yourself in the position of having to *decide how to decide*, and developing delegation assignments is one of those occasions. Specifically, you'll have to decide what means of delegation is most appropriate to the situation. These include the following:

- **Telling** – In this case, you decide what to delegate without input or consultation with anyone. This option can be efficient but should be reserved for the least experienced delegates. It can be successful when your individual decision quality is high and the likelihood of execution is high (i.e., orders are followed). Otherwise you risk a low quality result and develop very little ownership for execution.
- **Consulting** – Here you suggest a delegation but ask for input or improvements before finalizing your decision. This approach can improve both the quality of the assignment and the likelihood of execution. However, once you ask for input, be prepared to incorporate it into your plans. Otherwise, the next time you ask for feedback, you won't get it.

- **Collaborating** – In this mode, you develop ideas jointly for what tasks should be done and by whom. This option combines the ideas and experiences of all parties for a high quality result while developing ownership for subsequent execution.
- **Empowering** – With this approach, you let the delegate decide on their own what to do in order to achieve a specific goal. This option can be the best choice but should be reserved for the most highly experienced and strongly motivated individuals.

Except in special situations, I recommend the collaborating and consulting approaches because they tend to maximize quality *and* execution. They improve the quality of ideas because they call forth the different perspectives of the parties involved -- those of the experienced manager who should have the "big picture" and those from the on-the-ground subordinate who knows the situation firsthand. These two options also improve the chances for the most complete execution of the task.

Some new managers have learned that it's important to get "buy-in" so that people will want to do something. While there's nothing fundamentally wrong with this concept, it's limited and can even be seen by the subordinate as manipulative. The better term is "ownership," which Author Ken Blanchard says comes only from involvement.

The collaborative approach begins with brainstorming possible action steps to achieve a goal. To make this work, you have to set the stage and sometimes teach and demonstrate how to brainstorm. This approach fosters

"divergent thinking," the generation of ideas. It's helpful to begin this process by saying, "Let's brainstorm."

In this phase, all ideas are helpful; wild ideas lead to creativity; and no ideas are dismissed or criticized. It's important to get ideas from all parties involved, to build on one another's thoughts, and to think outside the box. You should remind everyone of the "Rules of Brainstorming," which include these:

- Quantity is better than quality
- Write down all ideas
- Never criticize an idea
- Build on the ideas of others
- Wild ideas are welcome and encouraged

The longer the list the better, but if the list ends up being a summary of your ideas, you're not yet using the collaborative approach. Ideally, you should not be able to tell whose ideas were whose.

> *"It's about helping each person have a role that is challenging as well as personally fulfilling. Do whatever you can to help craft that for each individual person. My experience with today's workforce is that a challenging and meaningful role, along with recognition, are the best gifts a manager can give an employee. It can mean more than salary, more than a title."*
>
> –Denise G. Kasper, Human Resources Director

Once the list is made, it's time to go back over it with "convergent thinking," the narrowing down of ideas to

viable and actionable next steps. Some of these will be your ideas made better by the subordinate's, and some will be a subordinate's idea improved by your additions. In the best case scenario, ownership for execution will be high because of the *involvement* you have generated.

If, on the other hand, the subordinate is not capable of generating ideas, is minimally knowledgeable about the task at hand, or is still uninspired to be creative, you may have to fall back to the consulting approach.

Consultation may also be your first choice if you need to make a delegation that is not negotiable but you want to improve the chances of a quality execution (e.g., a report needs to be submitted by a certain date and time). In this approach, you would state your delegation clearly but also seek ideas for improving upon it. Before doing so, you should be clear about what parts of it are nonnegotiable and which parts are flexible and open to creativity. I call this getting the subordinate's fingerprints on the assignment, and it goes something like this:

Manager: *I need you to submit an executive summary of your quarterly results in a written report to me by Friday at 3 pm. It's for the vice president and should not be any longer than five pages covering progress on goals, current strengths, weaknesses, opportunities, threats, and recommendations for the next quarter.*

Subordinate: *Sure. Whatever.*

Manager: *Since you're going to be doing it anyway, I was thinking this might be a good opportunity to do*

something special with the report and wanted to get your ideas on that.

Subordinate: *OK. What do you mean?*

Manager: *Well, we've talked about getting you some added practice with formal presentations to senior audiences and more visibility for the good work you do. Perhaps you could do something creative with the material to accomplish that at the same time. What ideas do you have about that?*

Subordinate: *Well, now that you mention it, it would be pretty easy to turn the report into a PowerPoint presentation as well.*

Manager: *Good idea. What then?*

Subordinate: *Then maybe I could present it to the vice president and provide the report as a leave-behind.*

Manager: *I'll see if I can arrange some time for you to do just that. What else?*

Subordinate: *It would help if I got some practice beforehand. Could I use some time at the Wednesday staff meeting and get some feedback from the team?*

Manager: *Absolutely. What if I can't get time on the vice president's schedule for a presentation this time? What's an alternative?*

Subordinate: *Well, I suppose I could still present it to the staff and learn from that experience. I could also turn it*

into an article for the intranet or maybe share the format so others don't have to reinvent the wheel every time.

Manager: *Sounds like a plan. Now let's summarize who is doing what here…*

In this scenario, the delegation was never an option, but the form it took and how it was executed took shape based largely on the input of the subordinate. As a result, ownership, quality, and likelihood of a successful execution were increased significantly.

Now that you've decided how to decide and gained at least some involvement in developing the plan, you have built the foundation for a very successful delegation. The next step is making things concrete.

> *"Most people talk delegation but don't embrace it fully. They delegate tasks but won't turn over the needed autonomy. Then they put in place excessive check ins and end up reworking it anyway. As a result, the manager thinks, 'Wow, I thought I was going to get all this done but I'm still doing it myself!' Your people aren't empowered; it's not their work. You are playing Mom for them."*
>
> —Trent Beck, Senior Manager

Deliver

Communication is a surprisingly complex process. Our brains are travelling at least 1000 times faster than our mouths can possibly move. Thus, we're easily distracted while we're talking and listening. Our ideas have to be filtered through our experiences and codified into language.

Then we have to send our message to another person through a channel, verbally, in writing, or electronically. In this process, the message has to be decoded, filtered, and processed through the other person's experiences.

What are the odds that our messages will be delivered unscathed to the receiver so that he or she hears them just as we intended? Very small. No wonder we need to repeat our messages at least eight times for them to be successfully heard!

That's why a good approach, a productive conversation, and a healthy brainstorming session don't yet constitute a successful delegation. The task has to be made concrete, and this may take a few iterations to get right. Here are some techniques for your consideration:

- After brainstorming, ask, "Out of that list, exactly what will you do first, second and third?"
- After delivering a delegation, ask, "Just to make sure we're on the same page, tell me again what you will do and by when?"
- After a discussion of the assignment, ask the subordinate to send you a message summarizing what he or she heard and is planning to do next.

You might think this is overkill, elementary or unnecessary, but you'll be surprised how different your perceptions are from the understanding of your subordinate. It's worth a few extra minutes to prevent hours of frustration later on. Even if you find out you were exactly on the same page, this step will increase accountability because the subordinate will have stated (or written) the expectations explicitly. Anytime

someone of integrity tells another person of integrity that they will do something, the chances of them doing it skyrocket.

Monitor

Just as "the job is not finished until the paperwork is done," the delegation is not finished until the checkpoints are in place. This phase has to do with setting milestones and deadlines, not just for the obvious sake of accountability but to help the subordinate to be successful.

New managers often shy away from this aspect of the process because they don't want to be "bossy" or be seen as "micromanagers," both of which carry negative connotations. If this is you, you may be fooling yourself once again, because assigning delegations without deadlines is like making a loan without collateral. It's risky for you and unsafe for them.

In addition to accountability, the top reason for installing monitoring mechanisms is to give the subordinate feedback so he can reach his goals. Honest and timely feedback is information from one event that has implication to a future one, a loop of output to input that keeps a system on track. It's neither good nor bad, it's just data. It's a tool. People have made the term seem negative or frightening, but

> *Feedback is information from one event that has implication to a future one.*

it doesn't have to be this way.

"On a cross-country flight from San Francisco to Washington, it's easier to adjust course in Las Vegas than to wait until the plane is half-way across the country. Give feedback soon; do not leave people on autopilot, especially for a 12-month evaluation period," said Bret Anderson. You don't want important delegations to go too far in one direction either, especially since it might be the wrong route to success.

Predetermined checkpoints are a non-threatening way to establish feedback opportunities and keep up the momentum toward the ultimate deadline. They also give you the opportunity to see whether the subordinate needs any help, resources, or a new "flight plan." Without them, you may be letting them fly too far off course.

> *"You know, it will cause more work in the short run, but you've got to facilitate their learning and experience. I saw the CPO [Chief Petty Officer] roll up his sleeves to turn a wrench one day, so I took him aside and said, 'Chief, do not turn wrenches. You have to let them break something or over torque it. You aren't always going to be here, and you have a lot of other work to do.' They enjoy their hands-on work, and they haven't gotten to the point where they enjoy moving people up even more."*
>
> –Ken Birgfeld, Airline Captain

There may be other reasons for a course correction, too. Circumstances might have changed for either one of you; checkpoints ensure that these will be surfaced and

communicated on a timely basis. Without them, you're driving a dynamite truck, setting staff up for failure, and putting your results at risk, too. If you stay in the dark until the deadline, it might be too late to get things back on track. Personally, I'd rather be guilty of a little micromanaging (at least the appearance of it) than letting my people fail because I was careless.

Nevertheless, I acknowledge that there is a legitimate concern about micromanaging in the delegation and review process, overdoing a good thing. It can quickly alienate certain people, and this is common among the latest generations entering the workforce.

But that's not a good reason for being completely hands-off in this regard. Establish your goals; set clear expectations; and install checkpoints early in the process. Do not "breathe down anyone's neck" or surprise people with spot checks. Doing so will demotivate subordinates and undermine results.

The following questions will help you bridge neatly into this phase:

1. What will you do?
2. When will you do it?
3. How will I know you are on track?
4. How will I know you are done?
5. What else do you need from me at this point?
6. What are you expecting to learn from this assignment?

Question #1 makes the assignment concrete. Questions 2, 3 and 4 bring about checkpoints and deadlines. Question #5

offers support and helps identify barriers that might need to be removed, and Question #6 turns the delegation into a learning opportunity.

> *"At first, I just did everything! As I moved up, I learned how to delegate, train and help others train. When I learned how and when to delegate, my job finally became enjoyable, and I cut my work week from 100 to 50 hours. I was also helping people reach their dreams, providing resources, and following up so they knew where they stood and needed to go. Then the job became a breeze!"*
>
> –Rory Sturm, Leadership Coach

On-the-job Learning

You are an expert delegator and invaluable leader when you can turn day-to-day assignments into learning opportunities. Time and talent are two universally precious commodities in business today. Furthermore, we know that leadership and other jobs are learned from experience. How do people get most of their experience on the job? Through delegations.

Only a lucky few get occasional job rotations, internships, preceptorships, and special projects. The bulk of what we learn comes from daily on-the-job experiences. Unfortunately, many such experiences are unintentionally wasted, lost and forgotten in the daily grind. However, you can resurrect this opportunity if you do the following:

- Always ask, "What are you planning to learn from this assignment?"

- Create and use individual development plans as a way of planning on-the-job learning experiences as well as formal training and development programs
- Match delegations to specific skill sets that need to be developed (see *For Your Improvement: A Guide to Development and Coaching* by Lombardo and Eichinger)
- Send every subordinate into their assignments with a purpose and a principle to learn or practice
- End every delegation with a reflection and a documentation of what was learned
- Demonstrate that you're always learning by taking courses, asking for feedback, and seeking developmental assignments

"People think they have to do everything themselves to be successful. They feel ownership and don't want to fail, so they won't chance anyone else having control over things. But a sharp manager will see that you are not developing your people, which is your real job."

–Jeffrey Bolea, District Sales Manager

As mentioned near the outset of this chapter, these skills are relatively easy to learn. It's the *will* to use them that may be the more challenging. This takes understanding the role, a developmental climate in your organization, and personal courage for you to step more fully into your management responsibilities. If you do, you will become a professional in your field, not just a do-it-yourselfer.

MISTAKE #3
ASSIGNMENTS FOR A SUCCESSFUL ASCENT TO MANAGEMENT

❑ Read *Leadership and the One Minute Manager* by Ken Blanchard and use this model to assess your team and lead team members situationally.

❑ Develop a responsibility chart that clarifies who on your team is responsible for what. Share this with your team and clarify it together.

❑ Conduct a strategic assessment of what your team needs to be doing in the future, so you know what skills to develop now.

❑ Illuminate the goals, interest and aspirations of each subordinate, and develop plans that help them reach their goals while accomplishing those of the organization.

❑ Revisit your team goals frequently to make sure they are still relevant and properly prioritized.

❑ Create an individual development plan with each subordinate aimed at the knowledge, skills, and abilities they will need for now and the future.

❑ When delegating assignments, consider how ready, willing, and able the delegate is for the task.

❑ Deliver clear expectations and concrete action items to help your associates achieve those goals.

❑ Increase ownership for execution by fostering involvement in making the plan.

❑ Create a developmental climate by turning every task into a learning opportunity. Use *For Your Improvement* by Lombardo and Eichinger as a guide.

*"Credibility is lost – not gained – when you pretend
to have all the answers and everyone knows
you don't and shouldn't."*

–Tom Davidson

Always Right
is Just Wrong

Making decisions without enough questions

Once upon a time, people got a job and they kept it. Not only that, they were loyal to their organizations, and their organizations were loyal to them.

I know it sounds like a fairy tale now, but it was true as late as the 1970s. But that all changed with globalization and particularly when downsizing began in earnest in the 1980s, when the unwritten "employment contract" between organizations and employees was shredded. As a result, people have changed in their outlook towards their work. They have had to become more independent, mobile, and flexible in their careers.

Imagine for a moment that one of the following happened to a friend of yours. Maybe they were a skilled customer service professional and their employer moved its service center from your hometown to India. Perhaps they were a successful sales representative, but their organization moved its business model online. Possibly they were an accomplished craftsman but the demand for their product or service declined to the point where they just couldn't make a decent living in the same field (like the buggy whip industry). In other words, they had to "reinvent" themselves.

Now imagine that they found a new job but in a completely new field of work. For example, the customer service professional became a legal assistant. The sales representative became a building contractor, and the skilled craftsman became a teacher.

What if one of these people turned to you for advice and asked: "What should I do now that I have a new job in a new profession?" You would likely reply with one or more of the following good answers:

- Find out everything you can about your new job
- Ask for help from your colleagues
- Work overtime to study your new career
- Learn what's expected of you and how people were successful there before you arrived
- Get the "lay of the land" so you don't step in any potholes or set off any landmines
- Get input from people who know this business so you can make the best decisions and don't have to start from scratch

Now imagine that the person "reinventing" himself/herself is you, because by becoming a manager, you *are* reinventing yourself. Would you take your own good advice*? Of course I would.* You say. *I'd be foolish not to.* I would agree.

Yet new managers make this mistake all the time. Rather than asking sufficient questions, getting advice from knowledgeable people, or involving their team in making important decisions, they don't' ask enough questions, acting like they already have all the answers. When this happens, they are making Mistake #4, "Always Right is Just Wrong!"

Unintended consequences

Unfortunately, this mistake discourages input, sullies reputations, and diminishes the quality of work. Quite often, the new manager is posturing to look good but ends up looking quite foolish, exactly the consequence they were trying to avoid. Several of the experienced managers I interviewed told stories about how they had to let a new manager "hang himself" to teach a lesson.

Willis Potts, for instance, said that he would watch decisions being made by managers who had not asked for input or help, knowing that the course they were on would have negative consequences. He weighed the pros and cons and would sometimes decide to "bite my tongue while they made fools of themselves," just to make a point and teach them a lesson about getting input.

> *"The wrong way is to be the only one with the ideas. That fosters the wrong environment."*
> –Jeff Samford, President

Ken Birgfeld, an Airline Captain, had a similar experience in the Navy. "If you take this too far," he said, "you squash creativity and people won't say anything in a meeting… people clam up and knowledge stops. The guys doing the work are the ones you need the feedback from."

Another unintended outcome of this all-knowing approach is that it sets the wrong atmosphere for collaboration. You are role modeling how you want others to behave. If you role model a know-it-all approach where you rarely ask for help, make too many decisions unilaterally, and pretend to never make mistakes, you're implicitly saying that this is the behavior you expect of everyone. Do you really want your staff acting like this? If not, then don't do it yourself. Otherwise, you'll multiply your own dysfunction by the number of people on your team and again by the number that they influence by their role modeling.

"New managers can be too dominant to start with (i.e., my way or the highway), which doesn't go over too well. This is true not only for new but for all managers. It causes problems in team building. They don't take the opportunity to get input from associates and other managers. Those who don't are going to miss a huge opportunity," said Don Sowder.

Carol Anderson said, "It's important to give people permission to ask questions, because if they think you expect them to know everything, then they'll avoid asking them. Questions are how you learn about the hidden issues and lurking problems, and those things that can jump up and bite you."

"It took me a while to learn that they are paying me to ask questions versus paying me to have the answers."
–Carol Anderson, Chief Learning Officer

The power of archetypes and stereotypes

Without really examining our assumptions, we adopt certain individual beliefs about what a leader *should* look like. These beliefs originate with our parents but branch out to include any number of people who cross our paths. They might include friends and family, ministers, politicians, sports figures, business tycoons, fictional characters, and military heroes. Each of these is a kind of archetype that affects our thinking at a deep level.

According to Jungian psychology, an archetype is a "collectively inherited unconscious idea," a pattern or model about how things should operate. For example, the idea that women should work solely in the home was a deeply held archetype that has changed very slowly. It was an idea passed down through generations and held firmly by a large percentage of the population. Even though this started to change significantly during World War II, it still took decades to make the shift more permanent.

Another example is the notion that organizations should be run in a hierarchical manner, where decisions are made at the top, orders are passed down, and lower echelons of employees are expected to execute the plans they are given. This business model follows a historical military archetype. It is one that has been challenged by contemporary organizations as a productive business model, and in some cases, even by the military itself. While there will always be

a need for hierarchy and bureaucracy, more entrepreneurial thinking is being encouraged and designed into the work systems of modern organizations.

Literature and movies use archetypes and paradigms to appeal to certain audiences or convey interesting stories. These can be powerful messages that selectively challenge or reinforce our belief systems.

A relevant example comes from the movie U-571 starring Mathew McConaughey, Bill Paxton, and Harvey Keitel. The World War II drama involves submarine warfare and certain principles of leadership. At one point, the junior officer played by McConaughey is thrust into the role of commanding officer, but he is indecisive, admitting in front of the crew that he doesn't know what to do.

Keitel's battle-hardened character, a master chief petty officer, takes the young officer aside and chastises him, saying "You have to know. You're the captain...you always know." Of course, the hero eventually rises to the occasion, earning everyone's respect and saving most of the remaining crew. While you might not have seen the movie, you know the message and have probably been taught this same archetype in other ways.

One of the reasons new managers make this mistake is because they have unwittingly adopted a mental model of what "good leadership" looks like. We learn, for example, *that leaders are supposed to know everything, and if they don't they are not qualified to be in their position.* Therefore

we think, *I have to look competent, even if I am unclear about the situation and have no idea what to do about it.*

The competence conundrum

Nobody wants to look foolish or incompetent, especially in the highly competitive world of work. As a result, people tend to hide the fact that they don't know everything, and try to show that they have it all together 24 hours a day. Thanks to nature and nurture, men appear to be the most notorious offenders.

> *"Of course it's hard to admit that someone else might know more than you do, but it values them and it informs you."*
> –Willis Potts, Vice President and General Manager

The old cliché that men don't like to ask directions has its roots in the fact that—well—they don't! I have to admit that there is something humiliating about having to pull over to ask a perfect stranger for help. Has anyone ever made fun of me for doing so? No. Has anyone ever remarked, "What kind of idiot doesn't know the best way to get back on I-295 from downtown?" No, I have never been chastised for asking directions, and I have always been helped. In fact, people tend to go out of their way to be helpful – *when you ask.*

Ah, but it's different at work, you say. *People there are just waiting for you to make a mistake so they can pounce on you, expose your vulnerability, and position themselves as the more competent one, truly worthy of accolades and*

promotions. This may be the case in a few instances, but it is not worth hamstringing your success on a daily basis.

"New managers believe they have to demonstrate their credibility and they can't show any weaknesses, like 'I don't know' or 'let me get back to you,' or 'I hadn't thought of that,'" said Larry Raynor. But these concerns are out of proportion to reality. It is true that there are a few people in every organization who will pass petty judgment, but they are insignificant in comparison to the number of folks who genuinely want to help you, especially if you sincerely ask for their help and listen to their advice.

> *"They believe that because they have been chosen for leadership they have to be the smartest guy in the room. As a result, they feel they need to prove themselves."*
>
> –Jim Horton, Sales Manager

Nevertheless, new managers will tend to hide the fact that they don't have all the answers, hoping to avoid embarrassment, beat the competition, or avoid letting someone down. After all, someone put them in this responsible position, and they need to prove that they made a good decision. As Donna Blatecky put it, "Someone put trust in me to be a manager, so therefore I don't want to fail them. You don't want to look bad or make a misstep."

It can feel like you are losing credibility when you admit that you don't know something. "It's embarrassing when there are things you are supposed to know and don't, and you don't want to admit it. You have to have a level of courage

to be able to say, 'I don't know that, but we'll find out together,'" said Robyn Bumgardner. The truth is that you will build more trust and credibility by this means than you can imagine.

This not only takes courage on your part but a level of maturity that is often lacking early in a managerial career. "It's better to go in like I don't know anything. I have to put aside old perceptions about myself and my function and learn. Admitting you don't know the answer, that you have to go out and find it, makes new managers nervous," said Sarah Gravitt-Baese. This kind of approach takes self-confidence in knowing that you may be giving up something in the short term (i.e., perceived credibility) for longer-term and more lasting gains (i.e., better results).

Nevertheless, new managers will tend to hide the fact that they don't have all the answers, hoping to avoid embarrassment, beat the competition, or avoid letting someone down.

Do you think a beginning juggler walks on stage without practice, expecting perfection? Of course not! The truth will be painfully obvious to those around you. You can't hide your incompetence. It's ludicrous and naïve to think you can.

Overconfident new managers are in a particularly precarious situation, not because they are any less intelligent or well prepared but because they will be less willing to show their

weaknesses. "Never let them see you sweat," is their motto. "Fake it 'til you make it."

"They are not ready to expose their weaknesses and insecurities. These are their associates but also their competitors," said Don Sowder. This is where confidence becomes arrogance and the downsides to a potential strength start to emerge. Appropriately self-confident managers will trust that enlisting people's help will build a more productive workplace. It takes maturity, experience, and courage to take this longer view, especially when the risks seem so high in the short term.

"People show up like they're king. Yet, it's so easy to ask questions, keep your mouth shut, and listen to what people have to say. It floors me that people don't do that. Here are all these people with a knowledge base you don't have, and they may have new information you can't possibly know. Something could have happened in the last two minutes. Not only are you missing an opportunity, but it makes you look stupid not to seek their help," said Ken Birgfeld. If you want to avoid this mistake, then you need the skill and, once again, the will to do so. The skills involve asking questions and listening, and having the courage to do both.

"At first I thought I had to have all the answers; then I realized that I didn't have all the answers. So then I went through a stage where I expected my staff to have all the answers, saying 'Don't come to me with a problem unless you also have a proposed solution.' That reduced the number of people coming to see me, but didn't help the organization. Finally, I realized

that often the best solution is found by working together to find it."

–Ken Allen, Non-profit Executive Director

Asking for help

Most new managers have been tactical to this point and all of a sudden their decisions have more far-reaching consequences. Everything is more complicated than it looks with many layers; things are more ambiguous. Yet they don't ask enough questions to understand the situations fully. It requires peeling back the layers and a much more complex thought process.

Questions are your most powerful tool as a manager but they are practically useless if you use them ineffectively or don't listen to the answers. To begin with, identify who is in a position to help you. This will include experienced subordinates and individuals in a variety of functions. "Get to know your support network and the resources available to you, like your HR partner, your finance person, and other experts. Almost everyone appreciates the acknowledgement that their discipline is valued, and it relieves you of having to be the expert in everything," explained Robyn Bumgardner.

"You have to solicit ideas from every single person, get their ideas, and facilitate healthy debate with the big picture in mind. The more you solicit, the more they will value the end product."

–Jeff Samford, President

Invest some time with these people during your "honeymoon period" in the new job. This is the relative slack time people give you at the start of any job, time to find the bathroom, tour the facilities, and meet your key stakeholders. Tell them in advance that you are going to need their help, and that you will appreciate their advice from time to time. Begin your education with them as soon as possible and set the proper tone.

Ideally, many of your questions should begin with "what" or "how" (e.g., "How does this process work?"), which solicits much more information than closed questions, which only require a "yes" or "no" answer (e.g., "Is this how you start up the machine?"). Questions that begin with "why" should be avoided, because they signal disapproval, convey an accusatory tone, and imply blame (e.g., "Why did you do it that way?"). While "why questions" may be harmless in their intent, you risk having a negative impact. In my experience, they can always be restated as "what" or "how" questions, which are much more likely to solicit helpful information (e.g., "What was your rationale for approaching the problem that way?").

Questions are your most powerful tool as a manager but they are practically useless if you use them ineffectively or don't listen to the answers.

In addition to types of questions, you need to choose what level of question to employ. The first level is more "big picture" in nature.

For example, the question, "What has been your approach to this in the past?" would likely elicit a broad description of how things worked previously. Spending time at this level ensures that you have the proper context before becoming more specific. These questions also make your probing questions more palatable, as the listener recognizes the natural flow from big picture to more specific understanding. If you jump to the next level too quickly, your inquiry can feel abrupt or contrived in some way. Also, by understanding the big picture first, your follow-up questions will be more on target than if you go too deep too soon.

"If you don't ask for help, you're winging it."
–Robyn Bumgardner,
Human Resources Professional

For instance, you might wish to learn more about the billing process, the customer service system, or how orders are filled. Secondary questions might be the following: "What has changed in the billing process since you started working here?" "What is working well with the customer service system?" "How are customer service orders fulfilled once they are received?"

The third level of inquiry is even more targeted and can easily feel awkward, invasive, or inappropriate without psychological permission or a series of precursor questions. For example, a logical third-level question might be, "What is one thing you would want to change about the billing process?" This is a very specific question, not only designed to learn something but to cause the recipient to think more carefully about their answer.

This is an example of a *powerful question*, one that can have significant impact. But these questions should be used carefully, after the context has been fully explored and trust has been carefully established. Such questions are generally short, provocative, and open-ended. Here are some more examples: "What did you learn?" "What is in your way?" and "What's the worst thing that can happen?" Asking for help generally involves the first two levels of inquiry; giving help often requires the third. "Learn how to ask effective questions but know it is also *how* you ask them. To draw out their expertise, without putting them on the spot, takes some finesse," said Ron Thiry.

> *"As a coach, I do see an over reliance on having the right answer rather than an approach that explores all the possible right answers."*
> –Mike McGinley, Vice President, Operations

The authenticity of your questions is crucial. Insincerity is easily detected by others, so asking questions in a perfunctory way, as if checking a box, will likely backfire. For instance, if you ask a question, then suddenly change the subject, explain where the other person's perspective is wrong or try to sell them on another point of view, then your intentions will be obvious as something other than genuine curiosity. Not only will you gain very little information, the person you asked will be much less willing to help you in the future, at least until you re-establish your credibility. If you want to have a sincere impact, then be sincere in your question delivery.

"Even if they ask questions, managers don't ask enough for help. I have asked others for their thoughts and their perspectives, but that was different from asking for help. 'Help' drives a different level of response. It's easier to ask for perspectives, but truly asking for help raises the bar," said Sarah Gravitt-Baese. In addition, it will take courage to make yourself temporarily vulnerable. Like adopting a learning mindset, it's a choice you need to make and live with.

> *"I would listen to what everyone had to say with my mouth shut. Don't ever show anyone the way you are leaning, then everyone will lean that way. It sets the tone as a predetermined decision."*
>
> –Ken Birgfeld, Airline Captain

Intense listening

Your willingness to ask for help and the quality of the questions you ask are useless unless you are also a good listener. In fact, your listening skills may be even more important, because people will be trying to give you information even if you aren't looking for it. "Listen more than you talk. If I had been given that admonition, it would have saved me a lot of heartache," said Jim Horton, Sales Manager.

Experienced managers learn this lesson in a variety of ways. I learned it in a public relations job for a paper mill. In this particular job, I met the public with complaints almost every day; I was the voice of the organization, often interviewed by the news media and public officials. Their concerns and complaints included job security, odor, noise, traffic, timber

harvesting, and even paint damage on their vehicles. I didn't get any significant training for the human side of this job, but I learned enough about mill operations that I could explain almost any problem from a technical standpoint.

But I learned a valuable lesson about listening in the process. People who are upset don't want a rational explanation or solution at first. They want to be *heard*. Not only that, they deserve it.

By the time people reached me with their complaints, they had to go to some trouble, taking time from their busy schedules, contacting the business in some way, and maybe being passed around more than necessary in the process. As a result, they were never happy and usually even more irritated than when they began the process.

In my naiveté, I would almost immediately start explaining the reason for the problem and offering solutions. The shocking thing was that no matter how politely or artfully I explained things, they would often go from being upset to being enraged within just a few minutes of my trying to "help." I knew I was doing something wrong when the most innocuous complaints turned into potential lawsuits right before my eyes.

> *"The most important thing I could teach is to shut your mouth and listen to those people who are doing what you are managing."*
> –Willis Potts, Vice President and General Manager

So out of desperation, I just started to listen to people, ask them questions that would get the whole story leading up to

their complaint, allow them to vent their frustrations, and show genuine concern for their troubles. Once I changed my approach, the results started to change dramatically. I could almost see the transformation when someone felt truly heard.

At some point, they would turn to me and ask calmly, "So what caused this problem anyway?" *Ah-ha! This is where I had been starting the conversation all those times before!* This became my signal that now was the time for explanations and solutions, and it transformed my listening skills.

Active listening is a mindset, not just a routine that can be easily followed or mimicked.

Sometimes I was even rewarded with feedback from the irate citizen who would say something like, "Wow. Thanks. That was the best conversation I ever had on the subject," and almost all I had done was ask questions, keep my mouth shut, and listen.

Looking back, I realized that people had tried to explain this to me, but until I saw it and felt it myself, I hadn't really learned the lesson. Once again, I found that knowing something in your head is not the same thing as understanding something in your heart. Reality changes with perspective, and perspective changes with every role.

The active listening skills you have read about or been taught (i.e., maintaining eye contact, using following skills to indicate that you are tracking what the other person is saying, reflecting back what was said from time to time, and

identifying the emotion behind the words) are just behaviors. Unless you are truly attentive, genuinely concerned, and authentically interested in the other person's point of view, the other person will not be or feel heard. So once again, active listening is a mindset, not just a routine that can be easily followed or mimicked.

> *"The greatest skill is listening and fostering two-way communication. You need to be able to hear what others have to say and be willing to modify your position based on that; if they don't trust you, you don't have a prayer."*
> –Willis Potts, Vice President and General Manager

If you think this is "soft-skill mumbo-jumbo," you are probably in the greatest danger of making this mistake yourself. Like many of us, you'll very likely have to learn this lesson yourself, probably the hard way.

But before we give up on you, please consider that this may also be the most practical skill you can learn. With an active-listening approach, you will save time, learn more, attract help, build better teamwork, and get improved results. It will help you get more done, stay out of trouble, and have time to work on more strategic problems.

Willis Potts put it this way, "Not valuing the input of those who are–on paper–less educated or less qualified is a huge mistake. They are good people, want to work hard, and want to help you if you approach it right. Just walk up and say, 'I'm new and ignorant about this,' then ask for help."

MISTAKE #4
ASSIGNMENTS FOR A SUCCESSFUL ASCENT TO MANAGEMENT

- ❑ Observe leaders and managers you respect, and watch exactly how they ask questions and how you can tell they are truly listening.
- ❑ Read *The Seven Habits of Highly Effective People* by Stephen R. Covey, paying particularly close attention to "seek first to understand, then to be understood."
- ❑ Practice listening by holding an entire conversation by only asking questions. You'll be surprised what you can learn.
- ❑ When asking questions, limit them to the open-ended variety versus the closed kind that require only a "yes or no" answer.
- ❑ Always begin your open-ended questions with "what" or "how," never "why."
- ❑ Monitor your own conversation style in meetings and assign a percentage to the amount of time you talked and the length of time you listened. Your goal should be 25 percent talking and 75 percent listening.
- ❑ Research the subject further and teach a class on asking questions and active listening.
- ❑ Make a point of explicitly showing that you have adapted your point of view based on someone's input.
- ❑ Encourage candor and truth telling. Thank others for challenging your thinking and taking the risk to speak up.
- ❑ Practice using silence rather than filling every gap with a question or a statement. Sometimes people need a little space to say what's really on their mind.

"Your need to be liked
will erode your ability to be respected,
and that will collapse the foundation of your leadership."

–Tom Davidson

Caught in the Popularity Paradox

Trying too much to be liked

A "paradox" is a concept that seems at first to be contradictory but eventually reveals itself to be true nonetheless. The subject of this chapter is the *"popularity paradox,"* the dilemma in which managers try so hard to be liked that they end up pleasing no one.

I've been a manager and leader for over 30 years now, including first-line supervisor, corporate vice president, board member and consultant, and this is still the hardest one for me. It has manifested itself over and over again in all kinds of situations. The good news is that I'm well aware of this tendency and work hard to keep it from being a derailer.

The bad news is that I didn't recognize it well enough or early enough in my career.

> *"It's not a popularity contest. You want to please everyone, because you think things will work better that way. But at the same time, the work has to get done."*
>
> –Jane N. Rothrock, Vice President

Near the beginning of my management career, my boss informed me one day that I was going to be promoted over a good friend, someone I felt to be quite deserving of the role and even better suited in many ways than I. While I definitely wanted the position, I knew the transition would be difficult for him and, subsequently, for me. Knowing this, my boss correctly clarified that he would communicate the change at the appropriate time and place.

You can probably guess what happened. Thinking that the news would be disturbing to my friend and deteriorate our friendship, I decided to preempt my boss' communication and "secretly" tell him myself. My naïve rationalization for doing so was this. *If I gently and privately let my friend in on the news, he would so appreciate my concern and compassion that he would still like me somehow if I softened the blow in my own way.* What I failed to fathom was the real consequence of what I was about to do.

After telling my friend the news, the first thing I learned was that I was right in thinking that he would be upset. Unfortunately, I was wrong about almost everything else.

After hearing the news from me and venting privately for a time, he decided to confront my boss almost immediately. As my short career "passed before my eyes," I followed him to my boss's office to see things through.

At least I was willing to let the chips fall where they may and face the music rather than cower in my cubical. After my friend dropped the bomb on my boss, I was invited to leave his office and be spoken with later. I did, and I was.

As a result of my need to be liked and my rookie decision making, I had managed to please *no one* and made a difficult situation worse. Instead of pouring cool water on the fire, it was gasoline, and I got everyone burned in the explosion! This was the "popularity paradox" in action.

> *"Some people aren't concerned with relationships but most human beings like to be liked. This is our tendency when going into a situation where we are not as confident as we'd like to be."*
>
> –Larry Raynor, Senior Director

No one, including me, could blame my friend for what he did. He had been passed over for an important job, blindsided by someone he trusted, and short-changed of the proper context and a full explanation. I didn't have the answers to his questions, and I was the wrong person to give them out.

My boss had done everything right, too. He had made a business decision based on many factors and planned his communications appropriately. Looking back, he was surely disappointed in me, but he wasn't surprised. He knew my

personality and the power of human nature and had foreseen what might happen, even warned me about it.

I knew at the time that I was learning something important, but in the blur of the event, it was hard at first to put my finger on all the principles involved. These friendships remained intact, and my boss continued to give me lots of chances to grow and learn. However, it would be years of similar bumps and bruises and dozens of interviews for this book before I realized what a classic mistake this had been. As a result, this error makes the list as Mistake #5, "Caught in the Popularity Paradox."

The Power of Human Nature
According to psychologists like Abraham Maslow (1908-1970), the need for approval and belonging is among the primary motivations of all human beings. Maslow's "hierarchy of needs" includes the following grouping of needs in the order of their importance to us. They are:

- Physiological needs like food and water
- Safety needs like security and health
- Love and belonging needs like friendship and family
- Self-esteem needs like achievement and respect
- Self-actualization needs like creativity and fulfilling our full potential

This model is often represented graphically in the form of a pyramid. In that form, physiological needs are in the primary position, on the bottom, and self-actualization needs are on the top. This illustrates the order in which humans seek to

satisfy one level of need, at least to some extent, before attending to the next.

Psychiatrist Karen Horney (pronounced "horn-eye," 1885-1952) catalogued a similar set of needs but arrived at a top-ten version instead. She also grouped these into three categories related to how we get what we need; she called these "coping strategies."

Her premise was that if her taxonomy of 10 needs were not sufficiently met, then people would seek to fulfill them in one of three potentially unhealthy ways: moving toward people, moving against people, or moving away from people. Her model is as follows.

Compliance (moving toward people)

- The need for affection and approval
- The need for a partner

Aggression (moving against people)

- The need for power
- The need to exploit others
- The need for social recognition
- The need for personal admiration
- The need for personal achievement

Detachment (moving away from people)

- The need for self-sufficiency and independence
- The need for perfection
- The need to restrict life practices to within narrow borders

Moreover, she showed that these coping strategies are established early in our lives, even as babies. As we learn these strategies and find them successful, they are reinforced as our preferred approach and become our individual *modus operandi.* Unfortunately, while we might unconsciously believe our approach is right and good, it doesn't always serve us well or get the best results. When this happens, our preference is likely being overused, "compulsive" in her terms, and therefore ineffective at times.

To be a successful manager, you must learn to recognize your particular modus operandi and choose the most healthy approach, which is often compromise (moving *with* people). In order to achieve this balanced approach, there must be communication, advocacy, debate, negotiation, and decisions.

The Need for Balance
Armed with a bit of insight in this area, well-intentioned managers stand a better chance of striking the right balance in some important areas. If I had known sooner about my tendencies, their implications, and my proclivity for relying on them too much, I might have managed things much better in the earlier example. I probably would have realized that popularity is not always in my control and that there are consequences for putting my needs ahead of others.

> *"I needed to be liked, even though I knew in my head that great managers are not necessarily liked by all. Those who are liked by all are not making the hard decisions. It's the old people-versus-task spectrum. I leaned toward making everybody happy, without*

enough emphasis on getting the work done. Then I was provided some feedback from my staff and others that I was not enough of a task master. It was an 'ah-ha' moment. After that, I started shifting to a more balanced approach."

–Denise G. Kasper, Human Resources Director

Just as any over-used strength can become a weakness, so can our over-used coping mechanisms. Look again at Maslow's hierarchy of needs and Horney's taxonomy. You might notice that some human needs are in conflict with others, even mutually exclusive. As the old English proverb states, we can't always "have our cake and eat it too" (i.e., eat our cake and still have it afterwards).

As Tom Chalkley, a Management Consultant, put it, "If you are a jovial, fun-loving or a sensitive person, you naturally want people to like you, but you can't have it both ways. The reality is that if you are too nice, the aggressive ones will use you, and the company will lose, too. The great ones can be both sensitive and firm at the same time."

You can spend your days "moving toward" people, as might be the case in the popularity paradox, but if others are busy "moving against" or "moving away" from you, you can find yourself in a contorted dance, finding little resolution. Sometimes we all have to be a little more or a little less compliant, a little more or a little less aggressive, a little more or a little less detached. Like many aspects of being a manager, striking the right balance is a life-long hobby.

"After I'd been promoted, I felt like I needed to be very, very serious all the time about work. I was supervising people older than myself and felt I had to show them I was a grown up. Then I got some feedback that showed me that everyone thought I was competent but not approachable, way too serious. I thought I had to rule with an iron fist, that they needed to be afraid of me. This was an epiphany that prompted me to smell the roses and enjoy the ride much more." —Jim Horton, Sales Manager

The Bank of Equity

Envision that you have an emotional bank account with each of your stakeholders. While this particular account does not hold money or anything with cash value, it does hold something of real and practical worth—a store of personal equity with others. With a complete stranger, you have zero personal equity, because you have no relationship. In fact, you have not even opened an account with a "minimum deposit!"

With new acquaintances, you may be granted some complimentary equity, depending upon how you met and by whom you were introduced. With a loved one or a long-time friend, you have certainly built a good deal of non-monetary value in your personal equity account. In either case, what happens to your account depends upon what you do and how you do it.

"The great ones can be both sensitive and firm at the same time."

—Tom Chalkley, Management Consultant

This account isn't just nice to have; as a manager, you must have it and constantly grow it. There are times when you will need to deliver some bad news, confront a performance problem, apologize for a mistake, or have a "crucial conversation." These events equate to writing a check on the equity account you have built up (or not). If you have attended to your investment with others, your equity account will be drawn down for a while, but you can build it back with care and persistence.

If you haven't invested adequately in the relationship, you will eventually find yourself with insufficient funds.

If you haven't invested adequately in the relationship, you will eventually find yourself with insufficient funds. When this happens, you will immediately be overdrawn, and your "check" will probably "bounce." This has penalties and is much harder to recover from than building the account in advance.

If this continues, your relationship might become irreparable; you might lose so much trust that the partnership becomes untenable; or you might alienate stakeholders to the point that one of you has to leave or be fired.

Confronting Performance Problems
One of the chief ways you will be writing checks of this kind is when you have to confront performance problems. This could happen at the formal checkpoints set up by your

organization (i.e., performance reviews), during interim reviews to help people stay on track, or absolutely anytime there is a need to correct a performance deficiency.

> *"New managers often use the shotgun approach when someone is not meeting expectations. They talk to the whole group instead of the individual, in private. They are afraid to talk eye-to-eye, so they speak in general terms to everyone. But usually the person has no idea you are talking about them, and if he is, then he is pissed because you called him out in front of his peers."*
>
> –Robbie Coleman,
> Manager of Maintenance and Engineering

While some managers confront performance problems annually, it is simply abdicating your responsibility to wait until that time. Interim and as-needed performance conversations are a must if you wish to maintain a productive balance in your bank account. By the time the annual performance review comes around, there should be "no surprises" for anyone. That's your goal—*no surprises.*

The popularity paradox will be foiling your effectiveness when you

- Rationalize that the subordinate does so many other good things that the problem at hand is inconsequential by comparison and therefore not worthy of discussion
- Avoid bringing up the problem, hoping that it will go away or diminish enough that it is no longer as visible to you or others

- Focus on the low performers, even though moderate and high performers need course corrections too, and will usually do much more with the information than the low performers
- Take such a tangential approach to the topic that the issue is really never clearly raised
- Address the entire team about a problem that only one of them is having, hoping that they will "get the message" without having to face them individually yourself
- Sugarcoat the matter by manufacturing good things to say, overstating them, or overstressing positives to the point that the truth is disguised from the unsuspecting subordinate
- Allow the same behavior to continue, without holding someone accountable to work standards, previous commitments, or other promises made, thus letting down both them as individuals and the team as a whole

"As a manager, one of the toughest decisions is what to do about people who are not performing. Clearly, an individual who is underperforming should be given a chance to improve his or her performance. However, sometimes it doesn't work. One of the mistakes I have made is keeping an employee even when it was clear that he or she was not going to be successful. Part of the problem was that I sometimes assumed that somehow I was responsible for their level of performance. After making this mistake a couple of times I learned two things. The first was that keeping an unproductive employee can be damaging to the organization. They

are not carrying their weight and, more importantly, the rest of the staff generally knows when someone is not performing. They wonder why there is a double standard. The second thing I learned is that I am not responsible for their lack of performance. As a manager you have to do what is in the best interests of the organization. If it is clear that someone is not performing and they are not going to improve—don't linger. Get them out of the organization quickly— don't linger."

–Ken Allen, Non-profit Executive Director

Looking back on my career, I recall times I needed to be more forthright sooner and to have more courage to confront in general. My tendency was to be so concerned about the other person's feelings that I would over blow their potential reactions in my mind, and sacrifice the delivery of the message. Jeffrey Bolea said something similar: "Most new managers want to be well liked, will write flowery field contact reports to make them feel good. But too much of this can backfire."

If you truly care about your people, then you will want to put their long-term goals (e.g., to reach a difficult objective, to get promoted, to change careers) ahead of your short-term ones (e.g., to be liked, to avoid conflict). When you understand this priority, then you are more likely to have the courage and learn the skills you need to intervene rather than let them drive off the cliff.

"Everyone has feelings, but some need more pressure than others. Regardless of the scenario, you need to

watch their self-esteem, learn how to step on people's shoes without scuffing their shine. In other words, you can apply pressure without destroying them."

> –Larry Raynor, Senior Director

As the manager, you are in a unique position help prevent failure for each of your subordinates. If they receive critical and timely feedback on their performance and still choose to ignore it, then at least you gave them fair chances to make course corrections and helped them adapt if they were open to your good help. *Yours* could be the last warning before they derail themselves, and if you shrink from this responsibility, then you are doing your staff a disservice and falling short of doing your job.

"Less experienced managers have difficulty with tough conversations, how to provide meaningful feedback. In the early days, I didn't give them specifics; I was too general, too soft, even when helping good ones get better. I still struggle with performance reviews, procrastinate on them. But I've gotten better at on-the-spot feedback, more informal but more immediate."

> –Ron Thiry, Vice President of Operations

Taking Charge

The popularity paradox is also related to the problem discussed in Mistake #7, "Popping the Clutch." New managers who take too long getting to know their people, building relationships, and making friends can unwittingly sacrifice results. If they wait too long to set direction, call for

change or otherwise "take charge," they may be getting caught in the popularity paradox.

Taking charge requires showing leadership that may make people uncomfortable, taking a position that may be counter to the popular viewpoints, or defending one's decision against overwhelming odds. An unwritten yet unavoidable condition of being a leader is that some people will want to reject your direction. However, you are unlikely to be taken seriously if you can't build a business case for your opinion, defend your position appropriately, and withstand controversy.

It is also necessary for the new manager to be unambiguous about his or her expectations. These are the goals that need to be accomplished and the key behaviors relevant to how the work should be executed. First, you have to know what these are, and second, you have to communicate them to others, both verbally and in writing. While this may sound harsh, it is actually one of the most compassionate things you can do. You will be doing everyone a favor by articulating these principles and making them explicit targets.

> *"Being liked and being respected are not the same things. As a manager, people may not like you or your actions, because it is not possible to please everyone. However, if you are fair and consistent, you will earn respect, which is far more valuable to you, your associates, and the organization."*
>
> –Carol Anderson, Chief Learning Officer

If your expectations are unclear, ambiguous, or shifting, then your subordinates are essentially shooting at a moving target, one that is hidden in a dark room. You can tell them when they don't hit it, but why waste time and frustrate everyone? Think about the reverse situation and you will agree. Make a target clear, turn on the lights, and get to business.

Leading Your Former Peers

More and more new managers I speak with report difficulty when they are elevated to supervising their former peers. Promotions within work groups have been a norm since "jobs" were invented. However, the newest generations to enter the workforce tend to put a higher value on maintaining friendships than those in the past. As a result, they tend to balance the relationship more than they should.

For example, to remain "part of the gang," the new manager is apt to continue hanging out with his or her peers on Wednesday nights (or the equivalent). While this can be fine on occasion, it has limited utility on the job.

In these familiar situations, informal banter can turn to disparagement of others, unprofessional remarks about the employer, or inappropriate expectations of the manager. When you are promoted over your peers, there is a need for some degree of professional separation. Being the boss and still acting like a peer causes confusion, a form of cognitive dissonance that does no one any good. Conni Morse calls it "being friendly without being obligated to be their friend."

"Many new managers fear separation from their established social network. When you started the trip,

you were a passenger, but now you are the driver. When you're driving, you have different concerns than the passengers. You have to be more responsible in a number of ways. You want to be both, but you have to be one or the other."

–Bob Scudder, Executive and
Career Development Coach

Taking Things Personally

As soon as you accept a formal leadership role, you attract the "slings and arrows" of others. Being criticized is part of the job. You may never come to like it, but you'll have to get used to it if you want to succeed. Even when you take initiative as an informal leader, you'll be resented by others. You become an immediate target because you threaten someone else's status and self-esteem.

Several group-development models bear this out. As teams evolve and devolve through predictable phases, they pass through at least one stage that challenges the role of leadership. In *"Cog's Ladder"* by George Charrier, for example, it is the "bid for power." In Bruce Tuckman's model, this phase is called "storming." The same phase is called "control" in the theories of William Schutz, and "counter dependence" in those of Wilfred Bion.

> *Being criticized is part of the job. You may never come to like it, but you'll have to get used to it if you want to succeed.*

Also recall that Karen Horney noted "the need for power" as one of her 10 basic human needs, and Abraham Maslow listed "self-esteem, achievement and the respect of others" as one of his five, so the dynamics of your new job are powerful forces that you need to understand in order to cope, survive, and thrive in the role.

Groups want strong leaders but when they get them, they harbor resentment toward them and challenge their authority. A common means of doing this is through criticism, both overt and covert. It is yet another form of the popularity paradox. You can't please everyone, and if you try, no one will like you very much.

Once you are promoted over your peers, your relationship will change, no matter how much you wish it otherwise.

"Being the hard-nosed boss is almost never the way to go. But managers will learn that they will have to make decisions that aren't popular. The goal is to be respected, not necessarily liked all the time."

–Joan Bendall, Vice President

Your job will require you to make business decisions that will sometimes hurt people's feelings. Experienced managers learn to keep this in perspective. Jane N. Rothrock, a Vice President, makes this point, "It's OK if people are not really really pleased with you all the time. Managers have to do the right things, and this is going to piss people off sometimes. Adults will come around if you've earned their

respect. If they like and respect you, then you can afford to have them mad at you for a day."

Once you are promoted over your peers, your relationship will change, no matter how much you wish it otherwise. They will see you and treat you differently, no matter how hard you work to remain their pal. You can't stop this from happening, so decide if this is something you can live with or not.

If not, you might want to take a leadership position with another team, department, or geography. Doing so will make it much easier and faster for you to avoid the popularity paradox and its repercussions.

> *"To be promoted within the same business unit is a classic difficulty. You can do it with great humility, but it's easier to be promoted to another unit where they don't know you."*
> –Dave Winter, Human Resources Executive

Like so many other aspects of the role, you must strike a delicate balance between positive working relationships and the professional detachment that you will sometimes need to do your job. When you do, you will be well-enough liked but even more respected.

Your truly important relationships will weather the inevitable bumps and bruises of the workplace (as mine did in the earlier example), and you can continue with the business of mobilizing your team in the pursuit of your mutual goals.

MISTAKE #5
ASSIGNMENTS FOR A SUCCESSFUL ASCENT TO MANAGEMENT

❑ Make a three-column list of behaviors you would likely see in a manager who is "well liked," "disliked," and "well respected."

❑ Discuss this list with an experienced manager or advisor, modifying the observable behaviors as needed.

❑ With the help of a knowledgeable third party, check the behaviors that you tend to emulate (or predict that you might) as a manager.

❑ Read *Emotional Intelligence at Work* by Daniel Goleman or take a course on the subject to better understand this body of knowledge.

❑ Take an assertiveness training class to balance your skills in this area if necessary.

❑ Volunteer for assignments that put you in touch with hostile audiences or angry customers. Take the requisite training and learn to cope with the negative feelings of others.

❑ Take a public position on something that is unpopular and advocate for your point of view even though you might come under fire for a time.

❑ Ask your manager to take part in the delivery of bad news. Get his or her help to prepare for the event and debrief your learnings thereafter.

❑ Take a class on negotiation, mediation or conflict resolution, noting tools and techniques to manage disagreement. Take advantage of role play opportunities as much as possible.

*"There's no point in having a team
if it doesn't harness diverse talents and perspectives."*

–Tom Davidson

Too Many Mini-Me's
Surrounding yourself with people like you

"Mini-Me," played by Verne Troyer, is the strange character featured in the Austin Powers movies and is the small clone of the notorious "Dr. Evil." While he isn't an exact duplicate of Mike Myers' character, he bears enough resemblance to the doctor in dress, mannerism and evil personality, that he lives up to (or should I say "down to") the name.

Dr. Evil and Mini-Me are a laughable analogy for a serious problem in the workplace, the perfectly natural tendency of people to surround themselves with like-minded peers and subordinates. Being surrounded by agreeable people can be a deceptively comfortable situation. Your tendency to do this is reinforced by the fact that your group decisions will seem expedient and without unnecessary complication. However,

it also leads to dysfunctional teams, bad decisions, and discrimination.

The Dark Side of Consensus

The consensus decision-making method has been highly touted and trained in the last few decades. While this has been a beneficial course in many respects, it has also become an overused and sometimes misapplied management technique. Organizations with a highly inclusive "meeting culture," run the risk of taking too much time to analyze and build consensus on routine matters, rather than using the consensus method selectively and deliberately.

A "good decision" is one where the group's resources are well-used, time is well-spent, and the decision is high quality relative to the information available at the time. A consensus decision can be just as bad as one made unilaterally.

Depending upon their experience and assumptions, new managers tend to have a decision-making preference, some shoot from the hip without asking enough questions while others are looking for consensus around every corner. As a leader, you must first decide how to decide, not fall into the trap of assuming that consensus, or any other method, is the one best method.

> A consensus *decision can be just as bad as one made unilaterally.*

New managers need to be particularly cautious of this fallacy and alert to the signs "groupthink." A term coined by William Whyte, author of *The Organization Man*, this refers to an unconscious group

decision-making norm where the participants avoid disagreement, minimize conflict, and bypass critical analysis in the name of cohesiveness and expediency.

A glaring example of this happened in 1986 when the space shuttle "Challenger" exploded and broke apart during launch. After the Challenger disaster, the Rogers Commission reported that NASA's organizational culture was a contributing factor to the accident because of known-but-overlooked flaws in certain O-rings and disregard for warnings on the day of the launch.

> *"If everyone is like you, then your outputs will not be as complete or innovative. This is what diversity is about. It is important to learn that everyone in your area of responsibility does not have to do it the same way you would do it. Take into account the attributes you have in your entire team and determine what else you need."*
>
> –Mark D. Cox, President/CEO

Jerry Harvey's "Abilene paradox" is a related condition. In this particular dysfunction, group members have trouble managing their agreement and unwittingly agree to some course of action that *none of them* thought was a good idea.

Dr. Harvey's anecdote for this was a family outing that originated on a front porch in Coleman, Texas. In the course of seemingly innocuous conversation, the group "decides" to drive to Abilene, Texas, for supper, something that none of the family members really wanted to do but – because no one objected – believed that all the others did support the idea. After a miserable day, the group reveals their true

feelings about the debacle, at first blaming each other then laughing at themselves for the strange result.

After reading Dr. Harvey's book, *The Abilene Paradox and Other Meditations on Management* or seeing his video (The Abilene Paradox) I have observed a number of groups become more cautious about their group process. Every now and then, someone will ask, "Are we taking a trip to Abilene?"

By surrounding yourself with Mini-Me's, you increase the likelihood of taking this particular journey because you will be minimizing dissent and squelching the voice of reason.

> *"If you think in terms of 'command and control,' you are likely to want compliance and pick people who agree or think like you do. If you think in terms of truly understanding and responding to the natural complexities of business, you will want to surround yourself with diverse perspectives to improve your ideas and solutions."*
>
> –Carol Anderson, Chief Learning Officer

Sycophant-icide

The visual image of Dr. Evil and Mini-Me is also reminiscent of another deadly disease, the "yes-man" syndrome. This is sycophantic behavior that is so fawning, unduly flattering, and ultimately self-serving that it is harmful rather than helpful. Like a trip to Abilene, it can be deadly to your decision making.

The new manager can unintentionally cultivate this problem by surrounding himself or herself with overly agreeable

supporters. As an individual contributor, you have certainly witnessed this behavior. But you may not realize that while this approach can be politically rewarding for some, it can also be fatal for the unsuspecting manager.

Naïve managers can fall victim to this disorder by letting their egos swell once they are put "in charge" of something. When this happens, a number of people will become more subservient, some more than others. Even your old friends and peers will treat you differently the day after your promotion, which should alert you to the pitfall. People who hardly gave you the time of day before will start to call you "sir," "ma'am," or "boss."

> *"Everyone is unique, and we try to make them all the same. When I selected managers, I would say, 'You've had lots of experiences in your life, which have you enjoyed and which have you not enjoyed?' This would give me an idea for how they would approach solutions so I could add different perspectives to the team."*
>
> –Mark D. Cox, President/CEO

Be careful not to judge their over-reactions too harshly, and be aware that your newly-acquired authority is simply a result of your job title. Don't let yourself think that your ideas are as genius as others would have you believe. You're the same person you were the day before your promotion (and even less informed about what to do) but with a title that has changed the dynamics around you.

Paradigm Paralysis

According to futurist Joel Barker in his book *Paradigms: the Business of Discovering the Future*, a "paradigm" is a model, a pattern, or a set of rules for how things work. We use them every day to function and solve routine problems. Paradigms may differ widely between cultures. But within cultures, we share similar work, political, family, social, sports, and dining paradigms.

For example, many of us use the same travel paradigm about getting to and from work; we drive, ride buses or subways. We have similar paradigms about work, pay, and benefits. Meal times are similar and the kind of food we eat is relatively comparable. Nevertheless, world travelers know just how much these paradigms shift with culture and geography.

A problem arises when a group of people using shared paradigms tries to solve new problems and get new results. When a paradigm becomes *the* paradigm (i.e., the way we've always done it), we can catch what Barker calls "paradigm paralysis." This condition exists when people using the same mental models filter data the same way and come to similar conclusions. Like anyone else, leaders can be effectively blinded by their paradigms, and the affliction is reinforced by being surrounded by Mini-Me subordinates.

A problem arises when a group of people using shared paradigms tries to solve new problems and get new results.

"It would be easier to hire people like me, but it wouldn't be effective. Everything would be a rubber stamp, but we would not have a creative conflict. I would have blinders on and would not be managing. I don't care how long you've been doing this, it's easier to stay in your comfort zone. But at some point, you learn that stepping out of it is essential."

–Karen Webb, President & CEO

One of Barker's many public examples of this involves the watch industry. The Swiss watchmakers' paradigm was to use tiny mechanisms, small springs, gears, and fine workmanship to produce the best watches in the world. They dominated the world of time keeping for decades.

Because they shared a paradigm, a successful one, the Swiss watch-making industry did not perceive a new paradigm for its craft, even though it was invented right in their own midst. So when the new paradigm, quartz crystals, was introduced to the world, the Swiss watch making paradigm became nearly obsolete. It took someone from outside their paradigm to recognize the data and capitalize upon it. In this case, that someone was Texas Instruments.

To help you filter data and solve problems to get new results, you need a diverse team. That means people with different kinds of education, experience, and points of view that are different from your own. In other words, not too many Mini-Me's.

"The problem is amplified if you have a technical background because you might not recognize the need for diversity of thought. Engineers tend to want to

surround themselves with people who think like they do. I finally figured out to have diverse individuals, including human resource people on my team with a totally different perspective from the technical one."
    –Willis Potts, Vice President and General Manager

Treasure the Dissenter

Remember that the reason we like to surround ourselves with Mini-Me's is that decision-making is more comfortable and expeditious that way. But according to paradigm paralysis, the quality of your result will be undermined. Does that mean that if your team is more diverse, you will be less comfortable and decision making more difficult? Yes, which means that you and your subordinates will have to learn some skills to cope with your diversity and leverage your differences. If not, you might as well remain homogeneous and settle for the same old results.

"Not everyone has to do it the way you do it. There are many ways to get the job done, so I will paint parameters for people to work within and let them get it done their own way within those guidelines."
    –Mark D. Cox, President/CEO

A great many resources are available to help with team effectiveness. You should be able to find appropriate team building tools, diversity training programs, and appropriate psychological assessments to foster your team's success. Check with your local human resource professional for internal or external resources in this regard. In the meantime, you should take all the advanced training possible in group dynamics, diversity, facilitation, and team leadership.

Also, add to your reading list, *Team Players and Teamwork* by Glenn Parker. In it, Parker provides a useful template for identifying and leveraging several team player styles. He shows that individuals tend to prefer one or two *modus operandi* and makes the case that teams need to have individual skills from all four styles to be effective. His team player styles are collaborator, contributor, communicator, and challenger.

According to Parker, "collaborators" are goal oriented and visionary, while "contributors" bring data, subject matter expertise and execution excellence to their teams. Furthermore, "communicators" are particularly concerned with team cohesiveness and positive work relationships. In Parker's model, the fourth style is "challenger," a style that can be extremely valuable but is also much maligned.

Challengers question goals, point out pitfalls, and disagree bravely and brazenly. While they earn a reputation for being contradictory and difficult to be around, they are often the conscience of the group and keep the visionaries grounded in reality.

> *"If you want to be a great leader, you have to create an environment where people come in and close the door and tell you what they really think. It's not always easy to create, but a team that challenges you will help you learn."*
>
> –Randy Wheeler, County Administrator

To guard against sycophant-icide, groupthink, the Abilene paradox, paradigm paralysis, and other nasty disorders, pay

particular attention to the last category above—the challenger. It will behoove you to find and foster disagreement within your team. People need to be willing to challenge your thinking and question your decisions, although not in a belligerent way and not all the time.

Don't look for this tendency or expect it from one individual, but spread the responsibility around and take it upon yourself at times. If you rely on one person to be the naysayer, they are likely to become ostracized by the rest of the group, and you'll get tired of their relentless criticism, too, not knowing when it was warranted and when it is just another rant! Teach everyone to raise concerns, reward them for disagreeing, and guard against being defensive when it happens. You can shut down the team for months with just the wrong words, facial expression, or voice inflection.

> *"As a new manager, you will have hiring and firing responsibilities. Always hire people smarter than you. Otherwise you will be dumbing down the organization with less and less qualified people."*
> –Kurt Frank, Vice President IT Portfolio Office

Choose Wisely

You may inherit your teammates at first, but you will soon have hiring and promotion responsibilities as well. This is your chance to alter, improve, and build certain team dynamics. Be alert to the kind of complementary skills and perspectives that will keep your team well rounded. Discuss the makeup of your team with trained observers and counselors who can help you see the pattern and determine complimentary personality types.

For example, if your team is comprised largely of engineers who think in terms of hard data and linear problem solving, you might look for team members who are more creative and think "outside the box." If your teammates focus on the details rather than taking a more strategic view of the work place, then you might need a "big picture" thinker. Should your group be composed of all white males with similar career paths, it will be an advantage to add people with a more diverse job history and life experience.

> *"People try to hire people like themselves, which is not a good thing. Most successful people hire a good mix of people who are not like the manager, looking for people that complement the team. They are not necessarily the same people you would hang out with but they need to be adept at bringing their complementary skills to the team, which is critical. None of us is alike."*
>
> –Kathy Stover, Assistant Vice President
> of Clinical R&D

You should always begin your search by defining the job-related skills needed for the open position. Industrial psychologies and human resource professionals can help you conduct simple or complex "job analyses." These are the backbone of your search for new associates.

However, when you reach the point of having a number of qualified candidates who meet your minimum standards, you will eventually have a choice regarding their "fit" on your team or in your organization. This is where you can choose between varied or similar backgrounds, creative or

traditional problem solvers, and familiar or fresh perspectives.

By diversifying the thinking in your work group, you can enrich the problem-solving process, encourage new ideas, and challenge the status quo.

A Final Warning

One final warning about surrounding yourself with Mini-Me's: It can have fairness and legal implications. The "good old boy network" is propagated by managers at every level who choose similar, traditional, and familiar people. This can mean the unwise and unjust exclusion of talented men and women of different ethnicities, religions, education, age, and national origin. Despite the changing demographics in the United States, this is still a persistent problem, and it can never be overlooked as a pitfall, especially for the novice manager.

Some of the biggest and most respected corporations on the planet have allowed this kind of discrimination, turned a blind eye to it, and encouraged it through their hiring practices and working norms. As a result, they have robbed themselves of the diverse talent they need to compete, gotten out of touch with their customers, and put themselves in ethical and legal jeopardy.

As a new manager, you have a responsibility to learn and follow the letter and the spirit of the law. Take steps at once to get basic training on employment law for supervisors. Start with the internal resources of your current employer, but don't stop there. This is your responsibility as well as theirs.

Also take the organization's training on effective interviewing and hiring procedures. Again, don't wait to be invited. If your organization doesn't offer any programs, look up "behavioral interviewing," and take a course yourself. Not only will you be protecting yourself and your organization from unnecessary risk, you'll be building a better team.

Finally, learn to embrace different points of view, encourage and manage disagreement, and cope with conflict when it emerges. Start taking group dynamics classes, shadow expert group facilitators in your area, volunteer to lead teams in unfamiliar parts of the business, and eventually train others in this artful skill set.

Eventually, you'll learn to be uncomfortable when there's *too much* agreement! You'll know then that you are no longer afflicted with the Mini-Me syndrome.

MISTAKE #6
ASSIGNMENTS FOR A SUCCESSFUL ASCENT TO MANAGEMENT

❑ Show your team *The New Business of Paradigms* by Joel Barker and *The Abilene Paradox* by Jerry Harvey, and discuss their implications for your team.

❑ Read *Team Players and Teamwork* by Glenn Parker and use his team player survey to build awareness among team members that varied styles are needed to achieve quality results.

❑ Take all the classes you can on fair, square and legal hiring practices, and/or consult with your human resources department for counsel and direction.

❑ Conduct a job analysis under the tutelage of trained professionals.

❑ Study and use "behavioral interviewing" techniques to illuminate needed skills, judge them objectively, and avoid unintentional bias.

❑ Form interview panels to minimize the chance of prejudiced decision making, improve the quality of results, and build team member support for the successful candidate during the on-boarding process.

❑ Encourage and reward dissenting opinions. Role model this behavior yourself, and modify decisions when warranted by new information or perspectives.

❑ Cast a wide net for future talent, looking for qualified individuals in all parts of your potential labor pool and generating the largest possible set of candidates who meet your minimum standards.

"Teams are complex organisms that require real dexterity,
not machines that can be slammed into gear."

–Tom Davidson

Popping the Clutch
Engaging your team ineffectively

One of my first real jobs was on the labor crew of a large farm, a plant nursery, near Gaithersburg, Maryland. On bad days, I cut chin-high grass and weeds with a long-handled scythe while dodging snakes and attracting ticks and chiggers. On good days, I enjoyed more interesting assignments, like transplanting trees, working in the greenhouses, or helping the landscaping crew lay sod and plant shrubs in the Washington, DC suburbs.

I quickly learned that the more skills I had, the greater variety of jobs would be available to me. So when I got a chance to drive the nursery's 10-ton dump truck, I jumped at it—even though I had never driven a standard transmission vehicle of any size!

I had watched "stick" drivers closely for years and was confident I could master the quick moves if given the opportunity. Fortunately, the truck was parked well out of sight of my boss and passersby, so I would not be easily observed or embarrassed as I taught myself the technique. On my side were miles of empty dirt roads on which to practice and a whole hour lunch break in which to learn.

If you have ever driven a manual transmission, you will likely remember your first experience. You depress the clutch with your left foot and start the ignition. Once the motor is running, you find the appropriate gear by wiggling the gear shift in various patterns with your right hand. When the stick is clicked into position, you simultaneously let out the clutch pedal while pushing down on the accelerator–the moment of truth.

If this maneuver is successful, you will ease forward and accelerate in the new gear range, at least until the engine's revolutions per minute (rpms) require you to face a new moment of truth into either a higher or lower gear. To go faster, you must repeat the process several times, always alert to choosing the right gear for the road conditions and desired speed. To slow down, you simply disengage the clutch, coast or brake to a stop, or downshift to a lower gear if you are not planning to stop right away.

When artfully done, the whole maneuver can be accomplished in a graceful second. Done properly, the driver and passengers experience the pleasant sensation of a minor-yet-exhilarating lurch into each new gear, best accompanied

by a smooth-purring engine. With the right vehicle, technique and passenger, it's the stuff of James Bond.

My first experience in that dump truck may not have been like James Bond's Aston Martin, but it was a wild ride just the same. My first attempt to engage the clutch was too forceful, causing the big rig to bounce forward while my head snapped back against the rear window; the engine died violently.

The engine stalled because I had "popped the clutch," released the clutch pedal too fast relative to the rpms of the engine. While this might mean a fast and exciting start for drag racers (i.e., "peeling out" or "laying rubber"), it's a rough ride for the rest of us.

If this had happened in traffic, I could very easily have hit something, hurt somebody, stalled in a precarious position, or a lot worse. But since I was alone on a dirt road, I tried it again!

Naturally, I was more careful on my second attempt, easing the clutch out slowly and revving the engine so it wouldn't die like it had the last time. While I could feel something happening, I wanted to avoid the bucking bronco effect this time and just ease into it. But this took way too long and filled the truck cab with noxious blue smoke that I found out later was from the disintegrating clutch pad.

It turned out that this more cautious approach had its own set of problems. When the clutch is timidly engaged, the flywheel of the engine and the clutch surfaces don't meet forcefully enough to grip, so they continue to spin, grinding

against one another until they are fully engaged or released. If this friction continues long enough, the timid driver can damage the entire mechanism without getting anywhere. Plus, you never forget the smell of that smoke!

True for managers, too
The analogy helps illustrate one of the major challenges that new managers face as they first start out with their teams. Like aggressive and cautious drivers, they often fall into two categories. On one side, aggressive new managers tend to "pop the clutch" by instituting too much change too fast, putting progress at risk, and potentially stalling the team needlessly. They can put unwarranted stress on the engine, and shake the passengers more violently than would be advisable.

At the other extreme, timid new managers tend to burn the clutch by being too cautious and slow when taking over their new responsibilities. This causes them to lose momentum, coast backwards, and make it harder to re-engage the workforce later on.

> *"You want to make your mark as a leader, but you forget that the people on the front lines know more than you do when it comes to what is working and not working well."*
>
> –Donna Blatecky, Deputy Director

As you search for the best combination for your situation, the new manager is likely to do some of both extremes. It's the only way to learn. While this phenomenon is experienced by managers at all levels, the new manager is particularly vulnerable because of his lack of experience and slowness to

adapt to the signals that he is being too abrupt or too slow to engage the workforce. While he is struggling to find the right combination, he is committing Mistake #7, which is engaging the team ineffectively.

Getting the feel of it

Just as vehicles come in all shapes and sizes, have special characteristics, and respond uniquely to driver movements, so do work teams, departments, and organizations. They each require a different approach in various circumstances. Some are more like high-performing sports cars that respond to the slightest suggestion from the manager; they can even be too responsive, go too fast, and have too many accidents. Others are more like the powerful dump truck, which can pull a heavy load but is unlikely to stop, turn, or accelerate very quickly.

In addition, each vehicle engages differently, some with very little pressure on the clutch mechanism, others requiring a "heavy foot." The gear shift itself might react to only tiny movements from the wrist rather than the big sweeping gestures that my first truck required. Finally, the engagement of the clutch mechanism itself might be more sensitive in some vehicles, causing the engine to stall out with even the smallest amount of poor timing.

Other vehicles are more forgiving, allowing the driver long moments of relative safety while the clutch pad engages the fly-wheel. The problem is that even if you're an experienced driver, you don't really know the nuances of the vehicle you are about to drive until you get in the driver's seat. Similarly,

the nuances of your team will not be immediately apparent until you get started.

Of this real-life phenomenon, Karen Webb observed, "One way is to go quick and direct, but the downside is that you will cut too much of the good in the process. Or you can go in passively, but then you're not giving enough direction. Both extremes are equally bad."

Maintaining a relatively high-performing work unit might require more caution. But turning around an ailing business unit under the pressure of time may call for a more aggressive approach; and you might be known as the turnaround manager. With more experience you will learn when it is appropriate to act more like a maintenance manager or more like the turnaround expert. But for 90 percent of your career, you will be striking more of a balance somewhere in between.

Too much too soon

Among my interviewees, clearly the most prevalent extreme was doing too much too soon, "popping the clutch" as it were. "When I was much younger, I had such an orientation for action," said Beth Egan Fedyna, Director of Sales Training and Leadership Development, "I thought the way you made a mark was to change everything and fast. Later I learned that the best way is not to change everything right away but to step back, respect others, and listen to their experiences in the job. Brainstorm what works and what needs attention to change."

Similarly, Ken Allen found, "One of the challenges for a manager coming into a new organization is how fast to

move. I have seen two different approaches. In the first, the new manager comes in and immediately begins shaking things up. In the second approach, the new manager takes time to learn the organization before making changes. I prefer the second approach. Regardless of which approach is used, however, it is critical that any changes be made all at the same time. Get them over with. If you don't, people will be forced to operate in an atmosphere of uncertainty— always waiting for the other shoe to drop."

The dangers of moving too fast include the following:

- Conveying disrespect for the workforce and what they have done well to bring the organization to this point
- Overlooking the cultural nuances of the business unit, thinking that if this approach worked once before it should work again in a new setting
- Alienating people unnecessarily by rearranging their work out of hand or ignoring their advice
- Discarding practices that were working quite well but were unfamiliar to you
- Overloading people with too much change, unrealistic expectations, or a workload that burns them out
- Disrupting the work flow to such an extent that the potential good is outweighed by the negatives of low morale, hard feelings, and disengagement
- Earning an immediate reputation as a hard-nosed manager with little regard for people and their past

Yet many new managers are promoted for their aggressive, energetic, and competitive natures. This often means they have a proactive and confident disposition as well. They

worked hard as individual performers and were rewarded with a chance at management. This is why so many err on the side of "too much too soon."

Military and corporate veteran Carol Anderson noted, "I've never seen heavy-handedness work well. I've seen new managers crash and burn because of it. In the Marine Corps, you could expect to change duty stations every three years, so you were taught how to do this right. One of the rules is that you don't go in making changes until you know what's up."

> *"You can't do it all and you can't do it now. I experienced a new school principal who came in and had to put his signature on the place right away. If we said the sky was blue, he said it was red. In one year, 13 people and 9 great teachers quit and parents were up in arms, all because he took control and made it his show."*
>
> –Jane N. Rothrock, Vice President

Some hard chargers make a career of the quick change. "Chainsaw" Al Dunlap may be the most infamous example, earning the nickname as a ruthless downsizer at Scott Paper and fraud perpetrator at Sunbeam-Oster. But while honest turnaround artists can be extremely valuable, their range and utility is usually limited. The problem is that once they get things going in a start-up or turnaround situation, they have usually damaged relationships so badly that they have a hard time "changing gears" to a more collaborative approach. The latter is often required to fine tune an organization and take it to the next level of performance.

"That quick, take-charge approach can be successful in the short run," explained Ron Thiry. "I've seen people do that and move on quickly, every year or year and a half, to stay ahead of their bloody wake. If you have a longer view, then I would recommend another approach."

Too little too late

"On the other side of the coin, some new managers try too hard to fit in rather than add value or make needed changes. There are powerful forces to make you fit in when you come to a new organization, to not ruffle any feathers or make waves. People forget that they were probably hired to make some changes," observed Dave Winter.

Similarly, Tammi W. Ellis noted, "My mistake was not making change fast enough. I was ultra-sensitive about where people were and not pushing very hard at first. I didn't brand it as mine quickly enough. I was sensitive to my predecessor's legacy and the staff's sensitivity to that," said Tammi.

The problem is that once they get things going in a start-up or turnaround situation, they have usually damaged relationships so badly that they have a hard time "changing gears" to a more collaborative approach.

With this approach, the managers may be trying too hard to fit in, tread too lightly on people's feelings, or wish to avoid

some of the conflict and anxiety that naturally come with a transition in leadership. They may also be concerned when leading their former peers, stepping into roles vacated by well-respected mentors, or joining a work group that has animosity toward the new boss.

> *"I saw things that were archaic but didn't want to rock the boat. Eventually, I did rock the boat but could have saved a lot of money sooner. I was afraid I might lose staff or might be penalized. It's easier to go with the status quo, but it's not necessarily better."*
>
> –Kathy Stover, Assistant Vice President
> of Clinical R&D

By going too slowly, problems are not addressed fast enough, people get impatient waiting for something to happen, and progress can stagnate.

The problems with moving too slowly include these:

- Creating expectations that little is going to change, so the likelihood for generating a sense of urgency is lost
- Letting the work unit find its own direction rather than fostering alignment in one new direction
- Missing opportunities to foster change at a time when it is expected and may be easiest to accomplish
- Underestimating the need and desire of the work group to embrace new or different methods
- Earning an immediate reputation as a push-over manager with a low sense of urgency or lack of confidence
- Allowing the work group to lose momentum, disengage as a team, or revert to individual priorities

Factors to consider

You will have to assess each situation carefully as you begin your new assignment and will surely have to make some adjustments along the way. During this period, you will be given some initial slack time by your team and your boss, commonly called the "honeymoon period." This can be as little as a few weeks for some first-line supervisors or as long as five or six months for executives with more complex roles and longer-term expectations.

Whether it is six days or six months, use it wisely. Talk to your peers, members of your work team, and your manager. Look at the personnel files, hold listening meetings, and interview customers at length (both internal and external). Get to know your people and technologies as fast as possible.

Here are some of the major factors that need to be assessed and considered when determining the right approach:

- **Size.** In general, small teams (up to 8 individuals) at one level can be joined quickly, and change can be affected more easily. However, this can vary widely with strong individual personalities and deeply held norms. Larger, multi-level, or matrix-organized teams (i.e., some of your team are direct reports while others have only dotted-line relationships to your group) will require much longer periods of time to join and adapt.

- **Capacity.** Some groups are more ready than others. They may or may not have the skills necessary to adapt to new demands, or they may not have the will to change. Leaders need to have a grasp of change

management, performance management, and human development principles to be successful.

- **Culture**. Over time, teams develop certain norms of behavior – positive and negative. This may happen on purpose or emerge spontaneously. Affecting the culture of your team can make a big difference. But it takes time and creativity.

- **Communication**. Effective communication has many facets. You can add or open more channels to convey information, improve two-way communication, time your communication more carefully, and use additional forms of communication, just to name a few.

- **Goals/Planning**. The clarity and alignment of short- and long-term goals need constant attention. In a team's history, these may have been clear, confusing, easy to accomplish, unreachable, dismissed as unimportant, or so rigid that they caused other problems. You should consider short- and long-term "what" and "how" goals of your unit and how they support those of the larger organization.

- **History**. Just like individuals, work groups have a history that affects how they view things, and this can be a help or a hindrance to moving forward. This may be particularly true if they have become jaded or unusually resistant for any reason.

- **Inertia**. If the organization is firmly entrenched in old ways of doing work, your team is less likely to adapt to sudden changes unless there is a significant threat to

their survival. This kind of work group may take more patience and require small wins to achieve momentum in a new direction.

- **Leadership**. Leaders have a profound effect on their teams, just by the choices they make in how they spend their time, what they communicate, and how they prioritize. One of the primary ways to affect a team is to demonstrate the behavior you wish to see in others. It is vital that a group's leadership team be in alignment toward common goals.

- **Policies**. For new managers, policies are usually given to them by their larger organization, but they may not have been followed in the past, or may need to be changed for a better future.

- **Procedures**. Work groups and teams have both formal and informal procedures for accomplishing their work. It is sometimes necessary to clarify what's going on before it can be improved. Also, groups are sometimes unaware that they are using dysfunctional, inefficient, or ineffective processes.

- **Recognition and reward**. Over time, pay and reward mechanisms can get in the way of good performance, and reward programs can undermine intergroup cooperation.

- **Relationships**. How well people work together is both an outcome of other factors and a force that can change the business.

- **Structures**. Managers can clarify or change reporting relationships, functional responsibilities, and decision-making authorities.

- **Stakeholders**. Key stakeholders in other parts of the business (or outside the organization) can have a tremendous impact on your success. These outside forces should be taken into consideration when determining and executing an approach.

- **Technology**. This tool has become increasingly key to how teams operate and includes both technologies that are central to the function of the business and those that keep people connected and communicating. The amount and sophistication of technology can have a role in attracting and retaining talent, and it can undermine relationships and communication if overused or substituted too frequently for human interaction.

- **Urgency**. Your approach may vary depending upon your evaluation of urgency, based on views from the work group itself, upper management, or outside forces.

- **Vision**. Every team needs a commonly understood vision so they are moving in the same general direction, making mutually supportive decisions, and avoiding counter-productive behaviors. The leader is responsible for setting, clarifying, and helping to translate the vision into actions and behaviors.

Getting it right

As you begin to work in your new team, you will be watched very closely by your team members. They will be trying to

assess their new situation and adapt accordingly. Generally speaking, they want a manager who

- Takes time to get to know people and how things work before they start making too many changes
- Has a clear vision for how they want things to be and communicates it clearly
- Lets people know exactly what he expects of them and finds out what they expect of him in return
- Involves people in goal setting and problem solving to the largest possible extent
- Establishes challenging and mobilizing goals on his own but then lets people determine how those goals are going to be reached

> *"Know what is really going on before you change anything. You might mistakenly change things that were working."*
>
> –Hattie D. Webb, Ed.D., School Division
> Central Office Leadership Team

"The first six months are important for gaining respect and trust, demonstrating how you are going to do things. It's not that you do nothing for six months, but you focus on early wins and relatively low-hanging fruit until you get a better handle on things," said Ken Robertson, Human Resources Director. Not only that, people have to know that you know what is going on before you try to change things, so making a visible effort to learn has side benefits as well.

Your listening meetings should be sincere, with your primary interest as learning the organization, its people, and work systems. However, a very important secondary benefit

is that people see and experience your interest in them, their practices and their history. This will improve the respect they have for you and lower the resistance you will inevitably meet when you institute change or ask for improvements.

When it comes time for change, you are looking for critical mass, not 100 percent support. You can expect 10 to 20 percent of your team to support you, your vision and your goals right away. About the same percentage will resent and/or resist your leadership and vision for the long term. The remaining 60 to 80 percent will wait and see what you do and how you do it before they explicitly support you or offer personal commitment to doing things differently.

People often use the word "buy-in" when discussing change and commitment. I prefer to think of leaders building "ownership," which implies more voluntary support and personal commitment. Buy-in implies that people are being sold something that they may not want. Ownership is earned and taken on voluntarily.

When it comes time for change, you are looking for critical mass, not 100 percent support.

"If they are not involved, the change will take a very long time or will never happen at all."

–Robbie Coleman,
Manager of Maintenance and Engineering

For people to really accept change, they have to be part of it. "Allow people to participate," said Robbie Coleman. "Allow them to be part of the solution, especially when there is going to be change. The people who are affected are the ones who most need to be involved in the change process. If they are not involved, the change will take a very long time or will never happen at all. People want to be successful, but if they don't own it, they don't care as much. If they are involved, they own it, they care, and they make it happen."

MISTAKE #7
ASSIGNMENTS FOR A SUCCESSFUL ASCENT TO MANAGEMENT

❑ Work with your manager to determine your "honeymoon period" and draft a plan for using that time to learn the system, assess people, and demonstrate who you are and how things will be.

❑ Meet with each of your staff several times to find out what is working, where the landmines are buried, and what they expect from you.

❑ Read *The First 90 Days* by Michael Watkins.

❑ Demonstrate that you're listening to your staff by making some initial changes based on the feedback you have obtained.

❑ Accept the fact that many current practices are good ones, even if you haven't seen them before. Don't dismiss them out of hand.

❑ Find out who can help you the most and who can hurt you the most. Get to know those people more than anyone else.

❑ Draw flow charts of the current business processes or systems as a way of understanding initially, but potentially as a way of improving later on.

❑ Find at least one internal mentor and one formal coach to act as sounding boards for your ideas and to help you think things through.

❑ With input from your team, develop an initial vision for work group.

❑ Achieve early wins that show initiative and keep up the momentum while you are still learning the system.

"One of the most attractive qualities of a leader is humility;
one of the most repulsive is arrogance."

–Tom Davidson

You've Arrived…NOT!

*Acting like the learning is over
when it is just beginning*

Mark Twain said, "All you need in this life is ignorance and confidence, and then success is sure." Other chapters herein are about ignorance; this one is about arrogance.

Twain's observation is funny because it is based on truth. People sometimes do go farther than they otherwise might because of their supreme confidence and the ignorance that it is founded upon. Yet these individuals usually have a third trait enabling them to pull the wool over people's eyes longer than they should, like political savvy, technical skills, or verbal dexterity. Without one or more of these, they are found out early; with one of these, they are found out later. In either case, they eventually lose their credibility and wonder what happened "so suddenly."

New managers sometimes adopt the perspective that they "have arrived," which has several negative ramifications, and no one is immune. First, it erodes the likelihood that they will be an active learner, which is essential to a fast start and on-going success in this role and beyond. Second, it makes them appear arrogant to stakeholders, who become alienated and less likely to offer help and support. Third, it reinforces the assumption that positional power is the primary approach to leadership, which limits their ability to mobilize people. To overcome this, the new manager must be humble and *learn to learn.*

The learning curve

With every new hobby, skill, profession, or job, we must all pass through the stages of learning, beginning with "unconscious incompetence." At this stage, you don't know what you don't know. This does not mean that you are untalented or ill-suited for the position. It means that you're new!

After some introduction to the unfamiliar task, you enter the next phase, which is "conscious incompetence." Recall the last new hobby you undertook. After you attended your first class or training seminar, you were far from proficient and even farther from excellent. You likely felt clumsy and uncomfortable until you got some practice and more advanced training.

One's first few dance seminars, golf outings, or ski lessons, for example, can be humbling experiences. What looks so graceful and fun when performed by practiced professionals, can feel awkward and even dangerous to you. At this point,

you are beginning to realize that you have a lot to learn. This is the learning stage where you now "know what you don't know," otherwise known as conscious in-competence.

In the third phase, you have learned a good deal more about the task, but the activity is still far from second nature to you. You have to *concentrate* on what you are doing and how you are doing it. After a few months of driver education, for example, and a year or so of practice behind the wheel, a teenager might be able to drive a car, but they have to pay particularly close attention to what they are doing to remain safe. This is the point of "conscious competence" or "knowing what you know."

As a new manager, your skills go back nearly to zero.

After more years behind the wheel, practicing your new hobby, or performing your new role, the activity becomes more second nature. You don't have to think as hard about the isolated movements and myriad of decisions. Activities are accomplished through "muscle memory."

Experienced adult drivers become so comfortable behind the wheel that they might travel for many minutes without really thinking consciously about what they are doing. You've experienced this feeling if you've suddenly become aware that you have driven for miles and don't remember passing familiar exits. This is the fourth and final stage of "unconscious competence" or "you don't know what you know."

"You just can't learn these things from a book. You are just going to trip up along the way; it's part of the deal."

–Tammi W. Ellis,
Executive Director of Organizational Development

As a new manager, your skills go back nearly to zero. Certainly you have learned some key principles in your early roles that will serve you in your new job (i.e., basic interpersonal skills, how to function as a member of a team, or analyze a familiar problem), but the level of complexity and the context has changed. The skills you have now will need to be developed further and new ones must be added. Some of your old tools will even become irrelevant or obsolete. You are at the beginning of a brand new learning curve. *You don't yet know what you don't know.*

Unfortunately, based on interviews and observations, the third mistake new managers make is to overestimate their skills and bypass critical learning moments, becoming defensive of constructive feedback, and turning away those who wish to help.

Learning to learn
After observing hundreds of new managers, I've noticed a trend that I believe is a reflection of their experience as a generation. To begin with, newer managers tend to be skilled with technology. This puts them at a clear advantage over their older counterparts in some arenas, and it adds to their confidence level to an exaggerated degree. Their false assumption is that because they are better at technology, they

must also have more prowess in other areas, like leading people and managing things.

In addition, they have high expectations, some of which stems from their upbringing and early career success. Many have been advocated for by their parents from an early age. "Soccer Moms" and "helicopter parents" had a big influence on this generation, and many have been treated as "gifted and talented" from before they could walk. Having suffered relatively little hardship, as a rule, they tend to have high self-esteem and low humility.

> *"They've arrived because of seniority or their fitness reports. They literally rose in the rankings, but I've seen plenty of guys in their position who were flexing their leadership muscles for the first time."*
>
> –Ken Birgfeld, Airline Captain

For high-performing individuals in the workplace, this mindset has been further exacerbated by constant praise from supervisors, high-visibility recognition programs, and monetary rewards that would make older generations blanch in disbelief. They also have an entrepreneurial spirit, which has made them impatient to advance and caused them to scoff at traditional "dues paying" during their ascent in traditional organizations.

The most practical outfall of this trend is that new managers don't realize how much they still have to learn. They are at phase one of the learning curve but imagine that they are at phase three or four. Over-confident management candidates see training and development opportunities as "boxes that

209

need to be checked," unnecessary hurdles that need to be tolerated, and trainers that need to be humored.

Adding to this dilemma, most organizations have very little patience for error. "Most organizations don't say, 'It's OK to fail,'" said Sarah Gravitt-Baese. "But the best leaders say, 'Look, you should feel nervous and anxious, but I'm here to help you develop and to help you focus on your team.' When these conversations don't happen, it leaves everyone vulnerable."

> *"Very often managers are anointed and told, 'Have a nice day. Why aren't you getting it done?' If you don't take time to let people learn, the results are usually less than stellar...you reap what you sow."*
> –Kurt Frank, Vice President IT Portfolio Office

The expectation is often one of perfection, if not immediate results. The daily evaluation by Wall Street analysts has driven a short-term mindset into corporations, and the public sector is under similar scrutiny to produce quick solutions to long-term problems. If public servants don't produce on single issues, they are thrown out of office. If corporations don't make their quarterly projections, they are punished in their stock prices. If new managers fail to get the prescribed numbers, they are sidelined or replaced. Judith B. Douglas warns, "You have to learn to learn, which means being willing to make mistakes. Fear of making mistakes is the bane of the new manager. Healthy risk-taking is an important way to learn new behaviors."

The learning organization is a more stable and productive model in the long term. Mike Bogenschutz learned that

learning was an expectation in such an organization during an interview process. He explained, "I was just making the transition to management when I had an interview that stuck with me to this day. Bill Raaths asked a lot of questions about what I did to improve myself, how I learned about manufacturing from outside the paper industry. I didn't have good answers. I was too busy to read. I was too busy *doing* to learn. I didn't think I had much to learn from other industries. *That's* arrogance. At the time I couldn't have told you two to three books I had read in years; now I read all the time."

"To be truly successful, you have to be able to look in the mirror and see yourself clearly. To do that, you have to let other people into the process. Get regular feedback."

–Randy Wheeler, County Administrator

Carol Dweck, author of *Mindset: The New Psychology of Success*, has identified two learning perspectives that people adopt in various parts of their lives. She describes the "growth mindset" where individuals see themselves as lifelong learners, works in progress, and seekers of learning opportunities. This makes them hungry for challenge, actively reflective on what they are learning, and thirsty for developmental feedback on their progress.

Alternatively, she describes the "fixed mindset" as quite the opposite, someone who feels naturally talented and predisposed for success. Unaware of their own perspective, they tend to dismiss feedback with any number of excuses or methods of resistance. They also disengage from the daily

process of observation and reflection. As a result, potential learning opportunities are wasted and time is lost. Clearly, new managers need to be in the growth mindset, but many are in the fixed.

Unless new managers can *change their mindsets*, whatever training and development they receive will have little utility, and they will miss other opportunities to learn on the job as well. As a naval officer, Bob Scudder noted, "I learned a lot from the people under me. I learned to look for the subtle feedback even before it was offered. I'd ask for feedback and look at the data even before I judged my own performance. Growth in one's ability to manage and to lead is a process of learning not blaming."

High performers usually have a strong *work* ethic, but few have the kind of *learning ethic* that it takes to succeed. "The most important skill is learning to learn, being open to feedback and new ideas. The hardest thing for me still is taking constructive criticism, but leadership is no different from any other athletic sport where you have to seek input and work on improving your skills over time," said Tom Mettlach, Operations Manager.

High performers usually have a strong work ethic, but few have the kind of learning ethic that it takes to succeed.

Lost humility

Some professions and organizations reward, in fact *require*, the highest degree of confidence, even arrogance. Combat aviators, for example, have to be sure of themselves. If they are not skilled *and* confident to the extreme, the enemy will have a distinct advantage, and this could be fatal. A similar "take-no-prisoners" attitude is also a hallmark of many risk-taking entrepreneurs, turn-around artists, and start-up experts. Think of Donald Trump and "Chainsaw" Al Dunlap, and you have a good idea of what I mean.

However, in their situations, arrogance is a necessary attribute. The best executives at this level know by intellect and experience when arrogance is appropriate and when it is not. Most would agree that impeached Illinois Governor Rod Blagojevich, convicted former Enron Corporation CEO Jeffrey Skilling, and imprisoned investment advisor and former NASDAQ Chairman Bernard Madoff appear to have crossed that line.

Extreme confidence is much less of a requirement in most organizations; however, it is still rewarded to some degree at very high levels. Nevertheless, I would advise against it as a new manager. You have not earned the privilege, and you will not be adept in its application. More importantly, it will work against you as a team leader.

> *"When I first became a manager, I was deliberately taken out of engineering and put into operations where I didn't know much at all. When I protested, my mentor said, 'You need to learn to learn from others,*

*and by doing that you will approach management in
the way you should.'"*

–Jim Horton, Sales Manager

Rarely do new managers show up with the swagger of a
Donald Trump, although it does happen. More common is
the new manager who feels confident in his technical
abilities, someone who feels self-assured that he can conquer
whatever challenge is laid in front of him. To a point, this is
a good thing. New managers need to be self-confident, but
they will not get far by crossing the line to arrogant.

By self-assured, I mean you have to be willing to speak up,
take a position, present to large groups, take pointed
questions, and defend yourself and your organization. You
also have to be comfortable enough "in your own skin" to
absorb criticism without becoming defensive, remain
flexible rather than rigid, and demonstrate openness to
alternative points of view. New managers can't be shy, and
they sometimes need to push back against the status quo.
You will sometimes have to swallow your pride. So a good
dose of self-assurance is needed for the role.

Nonetheless, a number of interviewees reported seeing new
managers with too much "attitude"; some had it themselves
initially but learned to temper it. "A young manager may
think, 'I'm the manager. I know best, and your opinion
doesn't count for much,'" said Kurt Frank, Vice President IT
Portfolio Office.

"One of the worst leaders is the second lieutenant in the
Army, the equivalent of the first-line supervisor in the
civilian world," said Don Sowder. "They actually know very

little because they are brand new in their jobs. The smart ones learn real fast that it is really the first sergeants who run the Army, and they had better pay attention to them. Yet it is the sergeants that salute the lieutenants, and their egos get in the way of the learning if they aren't careful," said Don. Carol Anderson, another veteran noted, "Gold bars will mean nothing to the Gunnery Sergeant who has been in combat. Similarly, managers who think that because they are a manager they don't need to listen to their employees will find they are losing touch with the realities of the organization, and losing respect at the same time."

As a new manager, you may also find that people treat you differently, more subservient, which can also inflate your ego. It's possible that some will be jealous or resentful of your new position, but others will be inordinately deferential.

If you allow your ego to become inflated, it will be immediately transparent to your team and detrimental to your leadership effectiveness.

"Their ego gets the better of them, and they think, 'Somebody thought I should be a manager, so I must know better,' particularly with their subordinates," continued Don Sowder. If you allow your ego to become inflated, it will be immediately transparent to your team and detrimental to your leadership effectiveness. As tempting and natural as this might be, new

managers must keep in mind that they are filling a different role in a very big team effort.

Admitting mistakes

The crux of the challenge is to maintain a healthy self-confidence level without being arrogant. To accomplish this you must begin with the right mindset, as previously discussed. In addition, you can do two major things immediately that will improve your learning and enhance your leadership impact on others. First, admit that you don't know everything and demonstrate this by asking for help, as noted earlier.

Second, recognize and admit your mistakes. It is not necessary to "fall on your sword" too often, but your willingness to step back and reflect on your own errors demonstrates to others that you are both secure as a leader and humble as a person, a winning combination for any manager. As Donna Blatecky put it, "You are building trust when you are able to admit that you made a mistake and admit it publicly. You have to let go of your ego to be able to say, 'You were right and I was wrong.' It builds trust."

"If people are not making mistakes from time to time, they are probably not working. They need to be told that mistakes will happen from time to time. The important thing is that we need to help them learn from those mistakes so they won't happen again."
–Donna Blatecky, Deputy Director

Tammi W. Ellis shared her experience this way: "Some managers have a hard time admitting their mistakes but this is so important for new managers. When I screw up, I just

march up and admit it, confess it, and take it as a lesson learned. This is not easily learned, and most new managers are even discouraged from doing it." Learn to take your mistakes in stride and people will trust you more, not less. In addition, you'll learn faster and make a less stressful transition to your new role.

The veil of authority

Positional power is undeniably part of your role, but the mistake new managers make is to rely on this method of influence too heavily when there are more collaborative and effective methods available to them. Of course, the leader needs to give direction, but the nuances of that go well beyond "telling people what to do." Naturally, the manager sets the course and holds people appropriately accountable, but that should rarely involve overt directive and negative consequences (i.e., command and control). The more effective leader generates a shared vision, makes a compelling case, aligns the organization's work with the individuals' goals, develops action plans with some degree of collaboration, encourages creative thinking, and provides balanced feedback.

> *Learn to take your mistakes in stride and people will trust you more, not less.*

Moreover, the extent of your true authority over others is minimal, especially with the more contemporary work force. "Another illusion I have had coming into management positions is that my ability to control things or people will

217

increase," explained Anthony Romanello. "What a disappointingly bad assumption that has been! The times I have used my authority as county administrator, deputy, and town manager can be counted on my fingers. Real power and effectiveness come from leadership, not from fear or coercion."

Simply ascending in an organization is nothing special. Your credentials are practically meaningless to your subordinates. They want to know who you are as a person, what you will be like to work for, and whether you can be trusted.

"New managers often feel entitled to automatic credibility. They don't know that they constantly have to earn credibility and trust. One newly trained manager I knew proceeded to put up his resume on the screen as an introduction to his new team, explaining why he deserved to be the manager. Of course, his credibility was immediately diminished rather than enhanced," said Bret Anderson.

People skills are paramount
Much of this discussion has to do with the relationships you build, and this boils down to your people skills. Ironically, "soft skills" are the hardest skills of all. Ken Allen noted, "I have a master's degree in government management, but the reality is often far different from the theory found in books. A key part of being a manager is working with people. You can't get that out of a book or a class; you have to *do* it. It's like being a parent; the job doesn't come with an owner's manual."

Some of the most gracious managers I interviewed shared stories about how they learned lessons about their

interpersonal impact and adapted over time. They might not have had the most finely tuned people skills to begin with, but they learned valuable lessons, often the hard way. While some of these attributes come more naturally to some than to others, it is possible to alter one's behaviors to the degree necessary to be an effective leader, *but you have to care about changing in the first place.*

"I was arrogant," said Jeffrey Bolea, District Sales Manager. "I was the manager and they were not. Thankfully, my boss sent me to two interpersonal skill development courses where I was slapped in the face for my pompous attitude. Before that, I didn't care about people's personal lives. I managed the sales rep, not the whole person. I eventually learned that if I managed the sales rep *and* the person, it would be a winning combination." In Jeffry's case, someone cared enough about him and his future to intervene. Not everyone would step in to prevent someone else's derailment like this, and not everyone would rise to the occasion as he did.

> *"The relationship piece of the business is incredibly important; there is no formula and no database. You are dealing with an asset that lives and breathes, laughs and cries, and you don't learn how to do that in a calculus course."*
>
> –Willis Potts, Vice President and General
> Manager

The growing body of knowledge known as "emotional intelligence" is further evidence that organizations are more fully embracing the importance of people skills in addition to

classic managerial training. Many of the large-scale reengineering programs of the last few decades have failed because not enough consideration was given to the human side of the equation. The field of project management and schools of engineering have incorporated the "human factor" in their curricula's core competencies for this reason.

Being proficient in this area requires all the basics, including active listening, being empathetic, and showing compassion. But it also requires more advanced abilities, like making someone feel *heard*, showing genuine respect for other people's opinions, and embracing many forms of diversity.

"You need to learn from your people," explained Robbie Coleman. "They want to be involved, show you what they know. This is especially true of Generation X. When there is a problem, I say, 'Come on; let's go look at it together.' That opens doors. It's both a way to learn and at the same time it shows that I'm willing to walk in their shoes instead of ruling from on high."

At work, you may be the supervisor on the organization chart, but in life, your subordinates lead full, complex lives without you. They raise families, balance budgets, serve on boards, lead their civic clubs, hold public office, and solve complex problems just fine.

"Never assume that you are smarter than anyone because of your job title," advised Dave Winter. "You need to know that the people you are supervising are at work only for part of their day. They have solved challenging problems in their lives without your help, and they deserve your respect."

If you have started to think that you "have arrived" (or someone sends you this book anonymously with this chapter highlighted), consider this your wake up call.

MISTAKE #8
ASSIGNMENTS FOR A SUCCESSFUL ASCENT TO MANAGEMENT

❑ Read *Mindset: The New Psychology of Success* by Carol Dweck and report the key points to your boss, your peers, and any direct reports you may have.

❑ Attend an assessment center or development center to "try on the role," get feedback, and find out what you don't know about being a manager.

❑ Volunteer at your local homeless shelter, food bank, Habitat for Humanity or church mission for roles that expose you to human hardship and offer humbling experiences.

❑ Be proactive about getting feedback from supervisors, direct reports, peers and customers. See whether your organization offers 360-degree feedback programs, and take advantage of them if at all possible.

❑ Ask people to show you their jobs, what they're proud of, and what they need from you.

❑ Take on roles where you know virtually nothing about the content or technology, forcing you to learn from scratch.

❑ Get to know your leadership tendencies by taking psychometric tests appropriate to business from qualified coaches or industrial psychologists.

❑ Interview managers and mentors you respect, and ask them what humbling experiences they have had and how these changed their leadership style.

❑ Study great leaders in history. Note their humble beginnings and how they learned from others.

*"It's wise and necessary to know your strengths
but lazy and naïve to ignore your weaknesses."*

–Tom Davidson

One-Trick Ponies
Can't Lead the Circus
Putting too much emphasis on strengths

The preceding chapters have outlined the eight most common mistakes made by new managers. While these findings were based on my own experience and those of a hundred successful day-to-day leaders, I believe them to be classic and relatively timeless challenges that face new managers in every sector of the economy.

My closing entry, however, speaks to a more transient issue, a currently fashionable trend in management circles, one that is appropriately well-regarded *but over used* nonetheless. I refer to the mantra of leveraging strengths to ensure greater individual success. I believe that the emphasis on strengths has gone too far.

The "Strengths Theory," fathered by psychologist Donald O. Clifton, was summarized in *Soar with Your Strengths* in the following way. He cited the fact that the Chinese had long been the Olympic gold medal champions in Ping-Pong. At the 1984 Olympics, the Chinese coach was asked about the team's training method. He explained that the team practiced eight hours a day perfecting *strengths*.

The emphasis on strengths has gone too far.

Asked to be more specific, he said, "If you develop your strengths to the maximum, the strength becomes so great it overwhelms the weaknesses. Our winning player, you see, plays only his forehand. Even though he cannot play backhand and his competition knows he cannot play backhand, his forehand is so invincible that he cannot be beaten."

Dr. Clifton's consulting organization went on to acquire The Gallup Organization, and his legacy lives on in further research, writings, and assessment instruments that bear the essence of this theory. His work probably reversed a negative trend of the 1950s, '60s and '70s that focused development almost entirely on "fixing" one's shortcomings. While our weaknesses may never be turned into strengths, the theory has been misused to our detriment.

The authors of *Soar with Your Strengths* made the case that students were expected to excel in all subjects rather than being allowed to fulfill basic requirements in some and focus on their areas of strength. This, they said, was tantamount to

offering "singing lessons to pigs." Their solution was one of balance: "Focus on strengths and manage the weaknesses."

While this is a sound premise, there is a dark side to its application. The principle has two important parts, leveraging strengths *and* managing weaknesses. However, the latter has been minimized and dismissed, because it is easier and more fun to focus on one's strengths. It's become an *excuse* for not dealing with shortcomings.

Olympics revisited

Revisiting a more recent version of the Olympics, compare the 2004 with the 2008 U.S. Men's Olympic Basketball Team. Both were full of NBA all-stars—the epitome of high performers with multimillionaire egos to prove it. The 2004 team was notorious for its strong personalities and unfulfilled potential, becoming the first Team USA to lose the gold medal since professionals became eligible in 1992.

The U.S. team had superior strengths, which they emphasized leading up to the games. They had the height, professional training, and championship coaching. Their coach, Larry Brown, was the only coach in history to lead seven NBA teams to the playoffs and the only coach to win both an NCAA National Championship *and* an NBA Championship. They should have dominated the field.

Apparently, *they* thought so, too. The 2004 team was so sure of success they strutted their MVP talent around Athens as if they were gifts from the Greek Gods and were guaranteed to take home the gold without breaking a sweat. Yet they were humiliated and finally set aside by Team Argentina, leaving them to grope for the bronze medal. Many Americans,

including me, rooted for them *to lose* because they were such an embarrassment to their country, not in medal counts but in behaviors. This team clearly did not "soar with its strengths." Rather, it wallowed in its weaknesses.

The 2008 squad, however, would deliver a different headline. Instead of the "Dream Team," they wore the unwilling moniker of the "Redeem Team." Their gold-medal win on August 24, 2008, was more than the redemption for which their country was hoping. But how?

Like the 2004 team, they had a proven leader of similarly impeccable credentials coaching it but using a different methodology. Mike Krzyzewski, Hall-of-Fame winning "Coach K" had led Duke University to three National Championships, 10 Final Four appearances, and 10 ACC Championships before being invited to the lead that year's team.

They also had the same kind of seismic NBA talent that characterized the 2004 team, even a few returning all-stars. They had the same height, strength, talent, NBA floor time, and adoring fans.

Nevertheless, the 2008 team looked different from the beginning. They were out supporting fellow Olympians in other venues for two weeks prior to their games, talking proudly about their country and their team in media interviews, speaking respectfully of the other teams, acting humbly about their place in history, and showing up on the court with much more than the same logo merchandise.

Their strengths were comparable, but their potential weaknesses had been on display four years earlier. Nobody liked what they saw, so they changed it.

Managing Director Jerry Colangelo and Head Coach Mike Krzyzewski took a more balanced approach, and so did the team. Ultimately, this would simultaneously leverage strengths and manage weaknesses. For example, this team was handpicked for talent *and* attitude. Among the hurdles, every prospect had to answer—in their own words—why they wanted to represent their country. There would be no pay or guaranteed playing time. The United States would not be a victim again of the can't-be-bothered elites and the last-minute resignations of the 2004 version. This team wanted to be there or they would be gone.

Building on this foundation, Colangelo and Krzyzewski engineered more than just playbooks and practice times. They kept the team focused on "the big picture," what they were there to accomplish—as a team. They even took time for "off-sites" together such as a visit to the Statue of Liberty and an exhibition game at Rockefeller Center. The team's official slogan? *United We Rise.* As a result, it was "in vogue again to be playing for your national team," said USA Basketball Executive Director Jim Tooley.

The 2004 team started practicing together just three weeks before the start of the Olympic Games. The 2008 squad made a three-year commitment this time, including regular summer practices and competing together in the world championships before their final exam. They practiced, shared playing time, learned from their mistakes, leveraged

each other's skills, and supported their teammates on the court and off. Even their uniforms sent a subtle message. "USA" was big and red on the front, while the players' names were a subtle blue on the back.

What Team USA did was exciting, but how they did, it was a spectacular example of Dr. Clifton's *whole* theory and better than the Ping-Pong analogy. In that example, the Chinese focused on their strengths to the exclusion of their weaknesses. In this one, they focused on strengths *while* also managing their weaknesses. It was harder, but it worked better.

Strengths Theory meets Self-esteem Movement

Much of the new workforce and, as a result, new managers of today have grown up in a time when their self-esteem was diligently protected for them, first by their parents, then their teachers, sports coaches, and even their employers. Unlike previous generations, they've had relatively little hardship along the way and met with immediate rewards and individual success at work.

Their loving parents had "blocked and tackled" for them from the day they were born, as first evidenced by those little yellow road signs that went up on automobile windows announcing the precious cargo—"Baby on Board"—as if the passing public needed to know or somehow cared what was in your back seat.

The same parents morphed into "Soccer Moms" (and Dads) whose mission was to get their bundles of joy into every after-school program, advanced-placement tutorial, and

resume-building club activity. "Gifted and Talented" programs were filled to over capacity, and grade-point-averages strangely soared past the maximum of 4.0.

Instead of winning and losing, baseball teams stopped keeping score so that the young players would not feel diminished. Sports banquets delivered trophies to every player, because they had all become special and it had somehow become inappropriate to promote the best and the brightest. The result has not been greatness but mediocrity, as proven year after year in the falling relative test scores of American students compared to children of other countries.

The next greatest generation was not yet through being prepared. Soccer Moms went aloft to become "Helicopter Parents" hovering close by their young-adult children as they went off to college and eventually took their first jobs. Not only did they rant against the umpires and coaches in Little League games, they did their kids' homework, bickered with teachers for extra points, blamed the schools for their lack of parenting, coddled their 19 year olds, and swooped in to solve relationship problems with roommates, boyfriends, and the campus police. Nothing was too good for their very special progeny.

This social tsunami started to break on the workplace in about 2005 when the little tykes and their gloating parents started showing up in tandem for their first jobs, enough to give human resource professionals the chills. Like college campuses, workplaces scrambled to adjust as mommies and daddies filled out job applications (as they had college applications), casually took seats at interview tables, and

clamored for 401(k) and other benefit information for their offspring when they arrived at work.

The parents themselves are slowly dropping from immediate view of employers, but the wake they left in the psyche of the next generation is keenly felt nonetheless. Old and new managers alike are coping with a workforce with an attitude, high expectations, and low tolerance for criticism, just the kind of place where soaring with your strengths is readily embraced but managing your weaknesses is just as quickly dismissed.

Rather than gird themselves for the inevitable shockwave, organizations played along for a while with high salaries, outrageous perquisites, high praise/recognition programs, and inflated salaries to keep their technical talent happy and loyal. But for the most part, they were not happy *or* loyal. They continued to change jobs in a heartbeat, put personal time ahead of business needs, and turn down promotions that did not suit their geographical preferences.

In this context, Dr. Clifton's theory was edited upon delivery. Instead of being received as sent—"focus on strengths *and* manage the weaknesses"—what got through the filters was only "focus on strengths." Any mention of correcting weaknesses is now often dismissed by the recipient as inconvenient, old-fashioned, or irrelevant.

Swinging the pendulum back to where it belongs

We all have to re-focus on both strengths and weaknesses, not to send the pendulum careening back to the other side

but to strike a better and more consistent balance for everyone's sake.

No matter what level you are in your business, leaders cannot rely on their forehands to the exclusion of their backhands. As managers, we do not have the luxury of the Chinese Ping-Pong champion, an individual player competing against discrete competitors one at a time with our "gifts." We need a large repertoire of skills to meet a wide range of situations that change by the minute.

No matter what level you are in your business, leaders cannot rely on their forehands to the exclusion of our backhands.

One-trick ponies can't lead the circus. In the same vein, expert musicians aren't necessarily *orchestra leaders*, and masterful accountants aren't automatically ready to be *department managers*, at least not until they widen their repertoires of skills.

Focusing on their strengths might make the musician a star performer on the stage or make the accountant a hero every time the books are closed. But these exceptional technical skills will *never* really qualify them to be leaders, even though the assumption is made every day.

We must be able to both manage the details and see the "big-picture." We cannot afford to be just good team players; we also have to be excellent team leaders. Our organizations do not need us to match our strategic wits with the CEO; they

need managers who can also reliably execute the plans that are already in place. We cannot get too comfortable with the status quo *or* "throw out the baby with the bath water" too easily.

As a result, individual performers and new managers need to grow into their roles. To do that, they need to be more open to criticism, failure, and mistake making. This way, they can employ both sides of Dr. Clifton's equation, start their development sooner, and learn faster. Middle managers need to be attentive to the development process, help quantify effectiveness, and intervene properly. And that means feedback, coaching, mentoring, and consequences. Senior leaders need to face the fact that their workforce has changed and adapt appropriately without overreacting or coddling.

Front-line managers don't have the luxury of soaring with their strengths just yet. They might have gotten this far because of their technical abilities, but these will not carry them through the next nine levels of management to CEO.

AFTERWORD

About the Author

Tom Davidson, CSP, PCC, SPHR is founder of Kinesis International, Inc., and president of Davidson Leadership. He is a leadership consultant, executive coach, and professional speaker. In private practice since 1999, he helps individuals accelerate successful transitions and organizations develop their emerging leaders. He also updates the skills of experienced managers to meet the needs of a changing workplace. His programs inform and inspire audiences with his sharp insight, practical advice, colorful analogies, and tongue-in-cheek humor on serious workplace issues.

Prior to launching his business in 1999, Tom spent over 20 years in the paper and forest products industry. During that time, he ascended from technical and staff roles in forestry and manufacturing operations to vice president of human resources and organization development.

He spent much of his youth in the great outdoors, thanks to his parents and the Boy Scouts of America, where his leadership experience started early. In addition, Tom has been a trail guide, a survival instructor, a firefighter, and a competitive windsurfer. His varied experiences and his fast growth as a manager are reflected in the training principles,

examples, and memorable stories he employs to make his points relevant and applicable to his audiences.

His formal education includes two degrees from North Carolina State University, a BS in forestry and a BS in agricultural economics. He later earned an MBA from the University of Richmond and an MS in organization development from The American University and NTL Institute in Washington, DC. He is also a senior professional in human resource management (SPHR), a professional certified coach (PCC), and a certified speaking professional (CSP).

Contact him at Tom@LeadershipNature.com to discuss your leadership development needs, new manager training, executive coaching, team performance packages, and keynotes speaking opportunities.

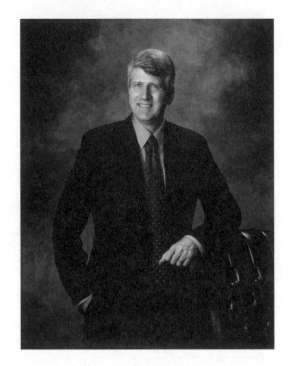

Tom Davidson

*"Organizations that don't support learning
from mistakes get the status quo they deserve."*

**RUMFORD
ACADEMY
PUBLISHING**

Order individual or bulk copies of this book
at www.RumfordAcademyPublishing.com
or www.DavidsonLeadesrhip.com

Learn more about our leadership development services and
products at www.DavidsonLeadership.com

New Manager Training
Executive Coaching
Leadership Team Tune-ups
Keynotes & Workshops

Specializing in leadership development for natural resource
professionals at www.LeadershipNature.com